SpringerBriefs in L

Expert Briefs

Series Editor

Helen Aristar-Dry, Dripping Springs, TX, USA

Springer Expert Briefs in Linguistics are invited topical monographs written by experienced linguists, designed to bring knowledgeable readers up to date on current linguistic subfields, approaches, or research questions. They are designed to be succinct overviews, restricted in length but unrestricted as to theory or branch of linguistics. Because of their brevity and expert authorship, they are well-suited to serve as unit texts in graduate and undergraduate seminars, as well as to acquaint scholars with recent developments outside their own research areas.

More information about this subseries at http://www.springer.com/series/15630

Margaret E. Winters · Geoffrey S. Nathan

Cognitive Linguistics for Linguists

 Springer

Margaret E. Winters
Program in Linguistics
Wayne State University
Detroit, MI, USA

Geoffrey S. Nathan
Program in Linguistics
Wayne State University
Detroit, MI, USA

ISSN 2197-0009   ISSN 2197-0017 (electronic)
SpringerBriefs in Linguistics
ISSN 2511-0594   ISSN 2511-0616 (electronic)
Expert Briefs
ISBN 978-3-030-33603-5   ISBN 978-3-030-33604-2 (eBook)
https://doi.org/10.1007/978-3-030-33604-2

This Springer imprint is published by the registered company Springer Nature Switzerland AG
The registered company address is: Gewerbestrasse 11, 6330 Cham, Switzerland

We dedicate this book to our teachers, colleagues, and students who have helped to shape our thinking as linguists.

Preface

Those of us who study language believe that linguistics, like other behavioral sciences (the French *sciences humaines* captures the nature of the disciplines), is an objective, data-based discipline. And we are, indeed, practicing our discipline in that way. What is perhaps occasionally forgotten is that we are doing so within the framework of some theory as to the nature of language itself. And a theory is just that: a set of hypotheses which each of us believes best captures all or most aspects of language in an overarching way, allowing for these data-based studies. Theories change over time, of course, strengthened as one or another of its hypotheses is proven to be true or discarded because too much has been disproven and replaced by better hypotheses.

We have opened this preface with some very basic notions in the philosophy of science ("theory," "hypothesis," "data") to say that our goal in this volume is not to change minds. Rather it is to lay out the basic beliefs of Cognitive Linguistics as a resource for those who base their work in other linguistic theories. Believing in one set of hypotheses (to state what should be obvious) does not preclude knowing how others think about language and how they come to conclusions, synchronic and diachronic, about how the many factors involved in understanding language may come together. What we hope to do is provide a short introduction, meant for fellow linguists and, perhaps, their more advanced graduate students.

Both of us have been practitioners of Cognitive Linguistics and involved in its development since its early days. Clearly, we think its conceptual framework is the right one. But, two things: first, we were not brought up (so to speak) in linguistics in the framework; Margaret Winters was trained in European Structuralism as practiced in Romance historical linguistics and Geoff Nathan had a mixed background including American structuralism, stratificational grammar, as well as far more mainstream generative theory. Secondly, perhaps stemming from this first point, we have over the years co-taught the history of the field; to do so, one touches on many theories as they flourished and/or expanded or were discarded over time.

One methodological comment is in order here. The SpringerBrief series is exactly that: a series of short monographs on relatively restricted topics. In one sense, this volume is restricted in that it is an overview, but it is an overview of a comprehensive theory of language crossing, many if not all subcomponents of linguistics. In many cases, therefore, we have provided a mere glimpse into some topics, although with references for those who wish to read further.

We would like to thank Helen Aristar-Dry who proposed to us that we write this book and Helen van der Stelt and Anita Rachmat of Springer-Verlag who have been guiding and encouraging us. We are also grateful to two anonymous reviewers who provided feedback on the proposal we submitted; they have helped to shape our approach here.

Detroit, USA   Margaret E. Winters
                                                                          Geoffrey S. Nathan

Contents

Chapter 1
Introduction

1.1 First Things

1.1.1 Cognitive Linguistics

Among the many ways in which linguistic theories might be categorized, one stands out for its simplicity. Theories, according to this metric, can be divided into those which take grammatical structure as basic and those which rather assign that fundamental status to meaning. For several decades, Generative Grammar in its many manifestations has been the key member of the structural category, while Cognitive Linguistics, although not standing alone, is certainly one of the most salient examples of semantics-based theories. Cognitive Linguistics directly contrasts with Generative Grammar in that respect, since it is a particularly successful instance of viewing Language with semantics as a primitive. A second basic division between these two approaches resides in their views of psychological reality. While both theories make strong claims about linguistic mental functioning, Generative Grammar on the whole sees it as a separate functionality, even to the point of positing an autonomous 'language organ' as part of the brain. Cognitive Linguistics, on the other hand, conceives of linguistic cognition as, for the most part, making use of the same functionality as other more general human cognitive phenomena, in particular, giving centrality to categorization.

As will be seen below, this conception has become the basis for a unified approach to multiple aspects of Language. Stemming from its claim of fundamental semanticity are analyses of units that are traditionally considered meaningless in more structurally-based theories, such as prepositions like *of*, and agreement markers and similar inflectional categories. It encompasses widely adopted views on the nature of metaphor and metonymy and their roles in the production and perception of non-poetic, everyday language. Related to these analyses are studies on the very nature of meaning and its cognitive underpinnings. Over time the theory has been expanded to

© The Author(s), under exclusive licence to Springer Nature Switzerland AG 2020
M. E. Winters and G. S. Nathan, *Cognitive Linguistics for Linguists*,
Expert Briefs, https://doi.org/10.1007/978-3-030-33604-2_1

both synchrony and diachrony, as well to all subcomponents of Language (phonology, the lexicon, and grammar), first- and second-language acquisition, and even poetics.

1.1.2 This Book: Its Nature and Outline

The present volume is intended as an introduction to Cognitive Linguistics for linguists who work in other theories and desire some insight into the nature of this one. We therefore do not explain terms which are shared across theories as would be done in a basic textbook. Our goal, rather, is to make this theory accessible to fellow linguists, colleagues who, over the years, have told us that they really mean to learn something about it when they have time. We do, however, envision the use of this volume, among other readings, in a course in comparative theories, certainly at the graduate level where students have already mastered the fundamentals of linguistics.

We will begin in this chapter by discussing the very name of the theory, reviewing variants and what they convey about the nature of the enterprise. The rest of this Chapter is an overview of the intellectual sources of Cognitive Linguistics which, as will be seen, vary geographically. Chapter 2 provides a survey of early studies, while Chap. 3 takes up the conceptual underpinnings of the theory. The subject matter of Chap. 4, the core of this volume, presents the application of Cognitive Linguistics across grammar, both synchronic and diachronic, as well as in phonology. Chapter 5 will provide an overview of relatively new approaches, including its application in acquisition, provoking a significant challenge to the generative 'poverty of the stimulus' account (Evans 2014), socio-cultural linguistics, and poetics. We conclude (Chap. 6) with some important questions which have not yet, we believe, been answered satisfactorily.

1.2 Naming the Theory

1.2.1 Earliest Names

1.2.1.1 Cognitive Grammar

One of the earliest references to Cognitive Grammar is to be found in George Lakoff's (Lakoff and Thompson 1975) paper where a case is made for a cognitive grammar, that is, one which directly represents human linguistic functioning rather than positing abstract levels and transformations: "… if one gives up on transformational grammars and instead assumes a version of relational correspondence grammars… we believe there is a direct and intimate relation between grammars and mechanisms for production and recognition" (p. 295). And again: "…abstract grammars do not have any separate mental reality; they are just convenient fictions for representing certain processing strategies" (p. 295). As will be discussed in the next chapter, although the term was launched in this 1975 paper with some of the underlying theoretical commitments, most of the theory was set out in the 1980s.

1.2.1.2 Space Grammar

At approximately the same time, Ronald Langacker published a paper on the English auxiliary (1978). In the first paragraph he states: "This analysis of the English auxiliary assumes a theory of linguistic structure called SPACE GRAMMAR. While this theory is still nebulous in many respects, and cannot be described in any detail here, I will note that it differs substantially from any established theory. It seeks a natural and integrated account of both form and meaning, the relation between the two levels being a function of the lexical or symbolic units which the language provides for the overt manifestation of semantic structures" (p. 853). In the concluding section he further says: "While I have assumed a framework I call space grammar, I have given only the vaguest and most fragmentary indication of what this framework might look like" (p. 881).

Unlike Lakoff's 'cognitive grammar', 'space grammar' is no longer the label for this theory or for any part of it, although Langacker and his students used it for several years after 1978. It was Langacker himself who explained his decision to abandon the name in the preface to his *Foundations of Cognitive Grammar* (1987: vi): "I initially called this framework space grammar. Why is not important—in fact, there are so many good reasons to so label it that an "official" explanation would only impoverish the expression's value. But despite its obvious appropriateness, a number of people have reacted negatively to the apparent frivolity of the term, perhaps with some reason." The term rather quickly disappeared from linguistic publications and, with the consent of Langacker as well as others, has been completely replaced.

1.2.2 Current Use

What is of interest is just how the title of the theory has developed. To the extent that we can tell, three terms are used for it, all based in English, but have been translated literally into other languages as the popularity of theory has grown. The three are 1. Cognitive Grammar, 2. Cognitive Semantics, and 3. Cognitive Linguistics,[1] listed here in what seems to be the order of their becoming labels. All of them call attention to the relationship with processing and producing language by users, so 'Cognitive' is a constant. The second term continues to vary.

As has already been mentioned, Lakoff (1975) was already using 'Cognitive Grammar' which was adopted as well by Langacker when he chose to abandon

---

[1]Construction Grammar will not be discussed here except to note the name which is something of a departure since 'cognitive' is not part of the title; see Chaps. 4 and 5.

'Space Grammar'. We surmise that the use of "grammar" was at least in part prompted by the fact that the theory arose in opposition to 'Transformational (or Generative) Grammar'; it would be natural to call attention to differences through the first half of the title and underline the opposition through this parallel construction.[2] 'Cognitive Semantics' is the first of two variations on the title, placing its emphasis on the fundamentally semantic nature of Language. Here too it is in contrast to the structure-based nature of Language claimed by generative linguists of almost all types (see below in Sect. 1.3 for a prominent exception). In short, Langacker's (1987) claim is that the basic nature of morphemes, words, compounds, and syntactic structures is that they are meaningful (having as well a formal—or phonological—pole). All of these units can be said to exist on a continuum of complexity where the differences are a matter of degree, not kind. Analyses are based, in turn, in this essential semanticity. Another point, also to be elaborated further in this volume, is that here semantics itself, in addition to its objects of analysis, is understood very broadly, encompassing what in other theories falls both within semantics and pragmatics.

Finally, the term 'Cognitive Linguistics' has become wide-spread without, how-ever, replacing 'Cognitive Grammar' or 'Cognitive Semantics'. It is used in the title of the major journal publishing work in this framework (*Journal of Cognitive Linguistics*, published by Mouton de Gruyter since 1990) and of the three handbooks (Geeraerts and Cuyckens 2010; Dabrowska and Divjak 2015; Dancygier 2017). We should note as well *The Bloomsbury Companion to Cognitive Linguistics* (Little-more and Taylor 2014) as well as *Introduzione alla linguistica cognitiva* (Livio and Luraghi 2003). The title is the broadest of those applied to the theory since it encom-passes phonological studies as well as those in other subfields of Linguistics, includ-ing Sociolinguistics, Psycholinguistics, and, most broadly perhaps, second language instruction and some literary studies with an emphasis on poetics.

The above paragraphs are not meant to be definite analyses or histories of the terms discussed, but rather a way of making some sense of the competing titles without overemphasis on their differences. It is our impression that the three titles, 'Cognitive Grammar,' 'Cognitive Semantics,' and 'Cognitive Linguistics' are used fairly inter-changeably in much of the literature; a recent issue of *Cognitive Linguistics* (2015) has reviews of *The Bloomsbury Companion to Cognitive Linguistics* and *Cognitive Grammar in Literature*, both published in 2014. We would suggest that the use of 'Cognitive Linguistics' for handbooks may derive from its use in the first and most widely read journal, with some attention to the notion that there can be—and are—cognitive approaches to most subfields of linguistics and related areas. Geeraerts (2010: 182), in fact, says that "[c]ognitive semantics emerged in the 1980s as part of Cognitive Linguistics," although in North America at least the term 'Cognitive Grammar' was most markedly in use at the time. 'Cognitive Linguistics', to repeat, has become a kind of generic umbrella term, although all three are still to be found in the literature.

---

[2]There has been some discussion about the use of "cognitive" in the title, particularly as a contrastive term, with formalists of many types pointing out that their work, too, makes claims about human cognition. The point will be taken up in Chap. 3.

1.3 Intellectual Sources and Affinities

Theories, of course, do not arise out of nothing, but are rather, to oversimplify, either reactions to or continuations of existing ones. In reality, as in the case of Cognitive Linguistics and most other instances, there is some of both, a reaction and a continuation, often with more than one predecessor to react against or continue. We will focus here on some of the multiple sources which have been claimed for the framework, stemming from aspects of various traditions. Since the earliest work comes from American linguists, we will begin with the rather short-lived theory of Generative Semantics (3.1) and parallel work in Cognitive Science (3.2). The theory spread almost immediately to Europe and resonated with those versed in prestructuralist semantic traditions (3.3), interacting with the more European complex of approaches to the philosophy of language. It must be understood that these paths of development are not straightforward; Cognitive Linguistics took some of its basic notions from those espoused by Generative Semantics, while simultaneously reacting against that theory. In the case of European semantic traditions, we really cannot speak at all about direct inheritance, but rather a rebirth of interest in some of the same topics (the role of metaphor and metonymy in linguistic use, for example). That being said, the rest of this section is divided into the three most recognizable threads.

1.3.1 Generative Semantics[3]

Generative Semantics arose within the transformational-generative tradition not as a reaction to the entire theory, but to specific aspects of it, usually captured in turn under the title Interpretive Semantics. The nature of deep structure was, in particular, called into question along with the place of meaning within the entire generative project. For the Interpretive Semanticists (those, including Chomsky himself, who stayed faithful to the original concepts of Transformational Grammar), deep structure is a template based on the grammatical structure of the sentence. Lexical choice, the result of the meaning to be expressed, is made late in the development of a given sentence, with words inserted into the syntactic structure. For Generative Semanticists, on the other hand, deep structure is meaning, and structure derives from this meaning. Meaning itself is based in predicate logic, not ordinary language semantics, so that, to cite a very well-known example, *kill* can be deconstructed into 'cause to die' (McCawley 1976).

The evidence for direct inheritance is mixed (see Winters 2015). The most important factor in favor is that, for Generative Semantics and for Cognitive Linguistics, semantics is basic and that the same kinds of analyses hold for the lexicon and grammar. They are both, in that respect, unified theories, able to account for linguistic data, whatever the size of the unit from the morpheme to the entire construction, by using a relatively limited number of theoretical constructs. Psychological reality

---

[3]This section is based on Winters (2015).

figures here too, as a strong commitment in Cognitive Linguistics (see Chap. 3 in particular) and as a somewhat more tacit claim in the earlier theory.

On the other hand, there are important differences as well. First of these is divergence in views on the very nature of meaning. As was stated above, Generative Semantics posited the rather formal framework of predicate logic as the basis for describing meaning, with more or less explicit claims for its being the way in which human beings produced and perceived language in real time; this claim for psychological reality was undercut in some ways by the very elaborate tree structures, often necessitating many layers, which were the hallmark of this approach. Cognitive Linguistics, crucially, takes the view that there are no layers to linguistic organization parallel to the surface and deep structure of generativists. Rather, everything is on the surface and meaning emerges out of the ways language users function, that is, out of what in other theories has been called 'ordinary language' as produced and perceived in discourse of all sorts. To be set out below (see 3.2 and Chap. 3), is Cognitive Linguistics's adaptation of prototype theory and the nature of the radial set (Lakoff 1987) as the basis for semantic (and hence linguistic) cognitive functioning.

As Lakoff (1987: 582) points out, some salient aspects of Cognitive Linguistics do not play a role in Generative Semantics. Among these are the importance of metaphor (and other semantic links like metonymy) to the later theory and the fact that Generative Semantics did not study the role of idioms. The first of these differences emerges from the basic polysemy of semantic units; if they have numerous meanings, then what relates the various meanings takes on importance. The earlier theory did not concern itself with questions of polysemy and therefore was not interested in how meanings were related. Idioms too require an analysis of how meanings interact, here within an idiomatic phrase instead of across meanings of the same morpheme or word.

Both Lakoff and Langacker practiced linguistics themselves within the Generative Semantics framework. They are not, however, in full agreement as to the degree of influence it had on their later thinking and the nature of Cognitive Grammar. Langacker (1987: 4 and p.c.) states explicitly that it is not an outgrowth of Generative Semantics, but shares that theory's view of the primacy of meaning over structure. Lakoff (1987: 582), on the other hand, does see Generative Semantics as a direct precursor of the later theory. In some ways it does not matter how founders view their sources; this is a matter for historians of science and perhaps with a greater distance from the material than founders can develop. However, it is of some interest that this difference, be it of degree rather than kind, informed Cognitive Linguistics from the beginning.

1.3.2 Cognitive Science

North American versions of Cognitive Linguistics benefitted from another important precursor. Categorization theory developed within Cognitive Science in the 1970s, most notably with the work of Eleanor Rosch and her associates (Rosch 1975; Rosch et al. 1976). The notion of a prototype category, which became central to Cognitive Linguistics, stems in great part from her work on the perception of color. Based on the data collected in the identification of colors in field work among the Dani people of Papua New Guinea, Rosch hypothesized that colors were categorized through mental images of the best instance of the color. She called them focal colors, influencing human thought through the prototype effect, the propensity to organize entities in this way. She further hypothesized that such color categories were structured. Not all instances of red, for example, were of equal status within the category of 'red'; rather, some were better instances, closer to the prototypical red and others were less good, perhaps closer to orange or to purple. Also deriving from this work is another kind of classification, basic and non-basic categories. If 'red', then, is the basic category, non-basic ones might be expressed as 'reddish' or 'red-orange.' The essential claim is a strong one about the nature of human cognitive functioning, that human beings classify relatively abstract physical concepts in structured categories around a prototypical instance.

Lakoff (in particular 1987) was one of the first among linguists to be influenced by this work[4] and adapted it to linguistic units, both lexical and grammatical. He rejected the notion of the unstructured Aristotelian category which called for absolute membership (an entity either was or was not a member and, if so, was merely one item on a list of members). Rather he adapted the Roschian graded category to even more abstract linguistic entities. Langacker (1987) was working in similar ways, looking at nouns and verbs as prototype categories and proposing ways that human cognition understood them. It is noteworthy this work, influenced by that of Rosch and her students in non-linguistic domains, did not call for specifically linguistic mental structures, but rather depended on more general cognitive functioning. Examples of this early work are to be found in Chaps. 2 and 4.

Categorization is not the only aspect of Cognitive Linguistics to be informed by Cognitive Science. Work on metaphor as part of every-day speech originated in literary and philosophical traditions and was explicitly incorporated into linguistics through Lakoff and Johnson (1980). This widely read book inspired, in turn, experimentation by Gibbs on the processing of metaphors, and in particular those which demonstrated the importance of embodiment to linguistic understanding and creation. Gibbs (2017) reports on decades of work, providing multiple examples along the lines of *dodging an issue* or *He'll be successful, but he isn't there yet.* Such work has, of course, through its experimental nature, strengthened the case for the theoretical constructs and commitments of Cognitive Linguistics.

---

[4]Labov (1973), working in a different framework, had already considered the interaction of words for physical objects ('cup' and 'mug') in what he called 'graded categories'. Stemming from his work on phonological variation, his intent in this series of experiments was to extend the application of earlier works to the lexicon. While the goal of this work and the framework in which it was carried out was quite different from what eventually became Cognitive Linguistics, the notion of structured categories was in the air during the last part of the 20th century.

1.3.3   European Prestructuralist Sources

When we turn to precursors other than aspects of Generative Semantics and Cognitive Science, it is particularly important to note the distinction between direct influence and affinities. No claim has been made that Cognitive Linguistics takes its views of semantics from the work of 19th-century linguists, but rather that those early linguist/philosophers and modern practitioners came to some of the same conclusions about the nature of language and meaning.

The Cognitive Linguistics claim of the essential meaningfulness of Language is a return to what Geeraerts (1997) and Nerlich and Clarke (2007) refer to as pre-structuralist notions, including the diachronic view of language change as meaning change and a focus, at that time, on polysemy. This wider historical approach was in itself a reaction against the earlier view that the lexicon and its development was studied as etymology, the history of words taken one by one. Rather the object of study was how meanings (not the individual lexical item) interacted with each other and served to allow speakers to interact with their world, both concretely and through metaphor and metonymy.

Underlying the notion of polysemy are two aspects of meaning, the onomasiological and the semasiological (Geeraerts 2010 with references); the terms are better known in European than in American studies. The former designates the branch of lexicography which considers how concepts are named (as manifested, for example, in the Word and Thing movement and in the construction of linguistic atlases). The latter starts with the word and its meaning to consider topics which touch on polysemy, synonymy, and the interaction of antonyms with each other. Both these approaches are reflected in Cognitive Linguistics, especially but not exclusively, in studies of the lexicon, both synchronic and diachronic. They provide a way of talking of polysemy and the relationship of meanings, either those of a single lexical item or through the (often pragmatically based) interaction of items to each other.

The work of French linguist Michel Bréal (1832–1915) is a case in point, as discussed in Nerlich and Clarke (2007). He coined the term 'polysemy' and saw the phenomenon as basic to language use, acquisition, and change. An evolution in meaning did not cause an older one to disappear, so taken synchronically, words have multiple meanings which users select through context. Bréal distinguishes ordinary use from the intellectual study of meaning; for him polysemy is an artifact known to lexicographers and other professionals, but is not present in the mind of users since they are guided in their choice of words and understanding of the choices of others by context. For him, then, polysemy is social as opposed to individual, an opposition which linguistics is still trying to reconcile. Cognitive Linguistics brings polysemy from the social to the individual (without denying what Bréal and others would label as social); the current theory's claim is that this very polysemy, present in our mental language capacity, informs our functioning as language users.

Geeraerts (1997) refers as well to the hermaneutic tradition, more closely associated in linguistics with Europe than North America. The basis of this approach is the act of interpretation; it has been applied most frequently to the disciplines of literary and religious studies. As a precursor to Cognitive Linguistics it refers to the ways in which human beings, through the act of categorizing meanings, are interpreting the words themselves, and the physical and epistemological worlds which provide context for understanding them. Radial sets then (explained in Chap. 3) take their psychological reality and functionality from this interpretation of meaning, not carried out at random, but strongly allied to the interaction of meanings and the varying relationships of related meanings to the larger mental world of the speaker/hearer.

To repeat what was said in the first paragraph of this section, neither Geeraerts, nor Nerlich and Clarke, nor the present authors are claiming 19th- and early 20th-century semanticists or hermeneutic scholars were direct sources of Cognitive Linguistics. Rather, they—and we—have reached some of the same conclusions on the nature of Language and of human linguistic functioning.

1.4 Conclusions

This preliminary chapter serves as an introduction to the theory of Cognitive Linguistics which emerged in the 1980s and has since become one of the most prominent semantics-based theories of linguistic function. As such it contrasts in multiple ways with generative theory, most basically in the primacy of the study of meaning, rather than structure in Language as an abstract entity and in the world's languages. Its development at the beginning involved the very name of the theory, with the framework for some early work entitled 'Space Grammar'. There is still on-going variation among 'Cognitive Linguistics', 'Cognitive Grammar', and 'Cognitive Semantics'. While each label refers to an aspect of the theory, probably the one which subsumes the widest number of subfields is 'Cognitive Linguistics', used in this volume and elsewhere to indicate that the theory has expanded beyond the relatively narrow area of grammar to phonology, socio- and psycholinguistics, acquisition, and even literary analysis.

While it is beyond the scope of this volume to talk in detail about the sources of the theory, we have considered some, albeit briefly. The most clearly defined is the theory of Generative Semantics, prominent as a challenge to Chomskyan theory in the 1970s. Of greatest importance is its view of deep structure as consisting of meaning rather than structure, semantic rather than syntactic. The approach to semantics, however, is based on the notion that the nature of deep structure is the same as that of propositional logic, rather than of ordinary language lexical meaning. Cognitive Linguistics is a further departure, since it rejects the idea of layers (deep and surface structure) of any kind and sees meaning in the more usual sense of the word.

Other sources should be called affinities or commonalities of reasoning. We can see similarities in approach with late 19th-century linguistics, and especially in the nature of semantics. During that century there was a change from the consideration of individual etymologies to the study of words in their relationship to the world and to each other, as exemplified by the work of Michel Bréal. It would be appropriate, we believe, to point to the aspects of Language that the Neogrammarians set aside as "psychological" (to be opposed to regular sound change, or diachronic phonetics, which they thought of as physiological) as part of this network of semantic precursors. As will be seen in Chap. 3 on the theoretical commitments of Cognitive Linguistics, a further basis is the Saussurian sign with form and meaning (a concept and the expression of that concept) sharing linguistic mental space (Langacker 1987: 76ff). For the most part, however, we must return to non-structuralist approaches for similarities to the current theory.

Before setting out the basics of Cognitive Linguistics as a whole, Chap. 2 will move from sources of the theory as set out here to how the earliest work took shape during the 1980s when the theory evolved and began to take on the prominence it has today.

References

Dabrowska, E., and D. Divjak (eds.). 2015. *Handbook of cognitive linguistics.* Berlin/Boston: de Gruyter Mouton.

Dancygier, B. 2017. *The Cambridge handbook of cognitive linguistics.* Cambridge, UK: Cambridge University Press.

Evans, V. 2014. *The language myth: Why language is not an instinct.* Cambridge, UK: Cambridge University Press.

Geeraerts, D. 1997. *Diachronic prototype semantics: A contribution to historical lexicology.* Oxford studies in lexicography and lexicology. Oxford: Clarendon Press.

Geeraerts, D. 2010. *Theories of lexical semantics.* Oxford/New York: Oxford University Press.

Geeraerts, D., and H. Cuyckens. 2010. *The Oxford handbook of cognitive linguistics.* Oxford Handbooks. Oxford/New York: Oxford University Press.

Gibbs, R. 2017. Embodiment. In *Cambridge handbook of cognitive grammar*, ed. B. Dancygier, 449–462. Cambridge, UK: Cambridge University Press.

Labov, W. 1973. The boundary of words and their meanings. In *New ways of analyzing variation in English*, ed. C. Bailey and R. Shuy, 340–373. Washington, DC: Georgetown University Press.

Lakoff, G. 1987. *Women, fire and dangerous things. What categories reveal about the mind.* Chicago: University of Chicago Press.

Lakoff, G., and H. Thompson. 1975. Introducing cognitive grammar. In *BLS*, 295–313.

Lakoff, G., and M. Johnson. 1980. *Metaphors we live by.* Chicago: University of Chicago Press.

Langacker, R.W. 1978. The form and meaning of the English auxiliary. *Language* 54 (4): 853–882.

Langacker, R.W. 1987. *Foundations of cognitive grammar. Volume 1, Theoretical prerequisites.* Palo Alto: Stanford University Press.

Littlemore, J., and J.R. Taylor. 2014. The Bloomsbury companion to cognitive linguistics. *Bloomsbury companions.* London: Bloomsbury.

Livio, G., and S. Luraghi. 2003. *Introduzione alla linguistica cognitiva.* Roma: Carocci.

McCawley, J.D. 1976. Lexical insertion in a transformational grammar without deep structure. In *Notes from the linguistic underground. Syntax and semantics Volume 7*, 71–80. New York: Academic Press.

Nerlich, B., and D.D. Clarke. 2007. Cognitive linguistics and the history of linguistics. In *Oxford handbook of cognitive linguistics*, ed. D. Geeraerts and H. Cuyckens. Oxford/New York: Oxford University Press.

Rosch, E. 1975. Cognitive representations of semantic categories. *Journal of Experimental Psychology: General* 104: 192–233.

Rosch, E., C.B. Mervis, W.D. Gray, D.M. Johnson, and P. Boyes-Braem. 1976. Basic objects in natural categories. *Cognitive Psychology* 8: 382–439.

Winters, M.E. 2015. On the origins of cognitive grammar. In *Change of paradigms–New paradoxes,* ed. J.E.A. Daems, 149–167. Berlin/Boston: de Gruyter Mouton.

Chapter 2
Conceptual and Historical Background

2.1 Introduction

When we consider the precursors of Cognitive Linguistics, what is striking is that, unlike the Kuhnian paradigm (Kuhn 2012), those who developed the theory were, in a sense, rebelling against themselves, not against earlier practitioners, their teachers and mentors. Ronald Langacker and George Lakoff were active participants in the development of Generative Semantics while early European practitioners, like Dirk Geeraerts and Rene Dirven, had, themselves, worked in the more philosophically-based semiotic approach to language. The present chapter will look at some of their papers.

It is the case, of course, that separating analysis from the theory that supports it is not an easy (nor, we would say, a desirable) task. There will be some overlap, therefore, between this chapter, whose focus is analysis, and the following one, which will abstract the underlying theory from later analyses and from the very early theoretical pieces discussed here.

2.2 The Initial Spark

2.2.1 The English Passive Construction

In the late nineteen seventies and early eighties a flurry of papers by Langacker, Lakoff, and their students introduced the general conception of Cognitive Linguistics to the world. Although, as mentioned in Chap. 1, Langacker first referred to the theory as 'Space Grammar', the fundamental commitments that formed the theory were already all in evidence in Langacker (1982). An earlier, somewhat obscure paper (Langacker 1979) contained some of the same ideas. Langacker (1982) analyzed the syntax and semantics of the English passive construction, perhaps because

© The Author(s), under exclusive licence to Springer Nature Switzerland AG 2020   13
M. E. Winters and G. S. Nathan, *Cognitive Linguistics for Linguists*,
Expert Briefs, https://doi.org/10.1007/978-3-030-33604-2_2

Chomsky's (1957) analysis of the passive was one of the strikingly insightful treatments that made generative grammar an early success. Langacker began with the fundamental Cognitive Linguistics assumption that *all* linguistic units, no matter how small (or, as we will see, how large) are meaningful. As he says, 'semantic structures are simply the conceptual structures evoked by linguistic expressions… all valid grammatical elements and constructs are held to be symbolic, in the sense of having both conceptual and phonological import' (Langacker 1990: ix).

Second, following from the fundamental notion of conceptualization, Langacker argued that grammar was symbolic of meaning, and that consequently linguistic expressions were ways to construe conceptual content. As he says, 'grammar provides for the structuring and symbolization of conceptual content, and is thus imagic in character' (Langacker 1990: 12). Because of this emphasis on imagery, Langacker has used visual images (specifically a kind of diagram to be exemplified below) to represent linguistic meaning in general. It is not that he intends to argue that all linguistic meaning is *visual* imagery, but rather that all linguistic meaning *is* imagery, which can be visual, auditory (as in phonological structure), or more abstract, such as the ways in which we conceive space and time.

Langacker assumed that the meaning of larger linguistic units was a function of the meaning of the units that made them up, plus perhaps additional meaning associated with the construction itself. The most striking difference between Cognitive Linguistic' view and that of generative grammar in this respect is that it forces the linguist to show that each item in a construction, including what were otherwise assumed to be meaningless grammatical morphemes, in fact does have meaning, and contributes to the meaning of the construction as a whole. While compositional semantics was not new (cf. Geeraerts 2010: 70ff on both American and European frameworks), what is important here is the rejection of the notion that the entire unit is nothing more than the sum of its parts; the structure, taken as a whole, contributes to its meaning.

There are consequences, however, to a strict application of conceptualization to all components of a construction and, in considering the passive, Langacker assigns meaning to the auxiliary BE and the past participle EN (not to mention the preposition BY). In doing so, he also introduces his trademark diagrams, intended to present a visual representation of the conceptual structure he is arguing for. His diagrams consist of a network of boxes (each representing some linguistic unit), but with markings on the box and within each one representing the unit's role in the discourse (e.g. figure vs. ground, which he has christened Trajector and Landmark), as well as what would in dependency grammar be viewed as 'valence'; that is, the linguistic/conceptual units that enter into construction with the unit in question. Thus, the perfect participial form (traditionally identified, since Chomsky (1957), as EN) has the conceptual sense of being the end point of a change of state, with the focus on the entity being changed rather than the initiator of the change (in traditional grammatical terms, the object rather than the subject). To illustrate with one of Langacker's diagrams, here is his illustration of one of the meanings of EN, specifically the adjectival use as in *swollen wrist* (Fig. 2.1).

The overall box encodes the linguistic unit. The circles are things, and the vertical arrows represent some process acting on another thing (referred to by Langacker

Fig. 2.1 Perfective 2

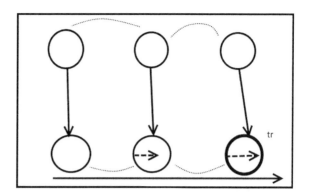

as 'energy flow'). The horizontal axis (in this case) represents the same objects at successive points in time (the dotted lines represent identity among the entities being represented). The small dashed lines in the bottom two circles represent successive changes of state of some kind. Finally, the fact that the bottom right box is darker represents that the focus of the overall expression is on the end state of this change of state brought about by the thing doing the changing.

His analysis of the past participle form at play in a prototypical passive construction differs from [perf2] in focusing on the entire 'box' without centering on one particular circle. However, its trajector (in other terms the 'figure') is identified as the recipient of the energy flow of the verb it is attached to (that is, it focuses on the 'object' of the verb in question). This 'figure-ground reversal' accounts for the traditionally-defined sense of the 'passive construction'.

Of course, in order to make the whole analysis work, Langacker must come up with an account of the meaning of *subject*, *be* and ultimately the *by*-phrase. And in the *Language* article that is exactly what he does.

2.2.2 Linguistic Gestalts

Somewhat earlier, Lakoff (1977) was, from within the background of Generative Semantics, laying out part of the theoretical background that would become Cognitive Linguistics. At the time, he wrote of *gestalts*, taking the term from a branch of cognitive psychology; now we would call them *linguistic units*. Among other claims Lakoff made was that gestalts are at once holistic and analyzable—that is that they are both the sum of their parts and more than that. What follows is a list of the properties of gestalts as Lakoff understands them: they "may bear external relations to other gestalts [and] may be viewed as instances of other gestalts. As a result, the parts… may get mapped onto parts of other gestalts or may 'inherit' properties of other gestalts" (Lakoff 1977: 246). Processes themselves may be viewed as gestalts (as Langacker does in reifying the meaning of EN). Gestalts may often be cross-modal, thus prefiguring a general Cognitive Linguistics view that linguistic meaning includes bodily and interpersonal interactions, as well as having grammatical, phonological, and pragmatic properties. Finally, gestalts must distinguish between prototypical and non-prototypical properties. As will be seen in Chap. 3, Cognitive Linguistics still retains most of Lakoff's characterization of units, although, in general, without the link to gestalt psychology.

2.3   Semantics of Grammatical Morphemes

2.3.1   Susan Lindner: In and Out

Once the commitment was made that *all* linguistic units had meaning, the first task was to take some of the traditionally 'meaningless' morphemes and provide accounts of their semantics. In Langacker (1991: 111–113) a preliminary analysis of English *of* is presented. However, over the early eighties several comprehensive studies were carried out of English prepositions that were not only meaningful in their own right, but also, crucially, contributed to the meaning of supposedly 'fixed, meaningless' idioms in which they participate (Lindner 1981). Lindner (1982) explored the meaning of *in* and *out*. She used versions of Langacker's diagrams to propose prototypical meanings for both *in* and *out*, then accounted for dozens of idiomatic uses.

Consider, for example, the discussion of *out*. Lindner was able to show that virtually every instance of the word was motivated semantically. Her demonstration used a number of conceptual tools that have become essential to Cognitive Linguistics analyses. First, she argued that *out*, like virtually all linguistic units in a language, is *polysemous*. That is, all the meanings of the word are semantically related, but not necessarily in the sense that they share a common 'underlying' meaning. Rather there is a central prototypical meaning (probably the one that immediately comes to mind first when the word is cited in isolation or if the context is ambiguous). However, *motivated* extensions of that meaning lead out in different directions, leading to a complex network of meanings, all of which are semantically related either to the prototypical meaning or to one of the extensions. This is the notion of radial category, which we will discuss in Chap. 3.

Lindner suggests that the prototypical meaning associated with *out* is of some focused object (*figure, trajector*) that is in motion from within some domain (the *ground*, or *landmark*) to some region external to that domain. The prototypical sense is illustrated by instances such as *She went out the door* (Fig. 2.2).

However, each of the elements of the schema of *out* can be varied in some way. For example, either the domain, the landmark, or the trajector can be understood metaphorically. The landmark could be something as general as 'existence' or the landmark could be a specific shirt:

1   He ironed out the wrinkle in his shirt (Lindner 1982: 308).

Fig. 2.2 Out

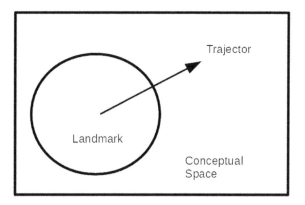

The landmark and the trajector could be the same object (this modification is referred to as a 'reflexive trajectory'). This alternative viewing (or, to use Langacker's technical terminology, *construal*) leads to uses such as

2   The stain spread out over the carpet.

It is also possible for the landmark to represent something like 'visibility, accessibility'. This would account for instances such as

3   The stars came *out* as the eclipse reached totality.

Here *out* 'codes a change of state from private to public' (Lindner 1982: 311).

Fig. 2.3 Out (become visible)

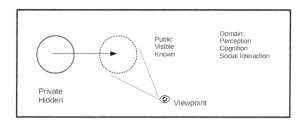

However, it is also possible for *out* to code 'sounds or sights becoming inaccessible to perception':

4   The street lights went *out*.

Finally, with both trajector and landmark interpreted metaphorically, the senses in (3) and (4) could even occur in a single sentence:

5   Dredge *out* a fact from memory and later blot it *out* (Lindner 1982: 312).

2.3.2 *Claudia Brugman:* Over

At about the same time, Brugman (1981, 1988) performed a similar analysis of *over*, again illustrating the point that what had generally been thought of as 'meaningless' uses of such morphemes were all semantically contentful, and related in motivated ways to the prototypical sense of the word or morpheme in question. Thus, Brugman was able to show that uses such as

6   Mary turned *over* a rock
7   The Picasso hung *over* the fireplace
8   Bill is so *over* his girlfriend
9   It's time to do this play *over*.

could all be motivated in the same way that *out* was treated. It is important to realize that the goal for each of these analyses was to account for *every* distinct sense of these morphemes in a plausible, semantically-motivated fashion.

2.4 The Ordinary Language Use of Metaphor

Almost certainly the most influential work in this early period was Lakoff and Johnson (1980), authored jointly by George Lakoff, a linguist, and Mark Johnson, a philosopher. In it they argued that metaphor, generally thought of as a recherché literary ornament, pervaded ordinary language in virtually every aspect. What Lakoff and Johnson argue is that metaphors are the way that our cognition understands abstract notions—by mapping more abstract concepts onto more physical notions. For example, English (and many other languages) understands *quantity* as being mapped onto *vertical orientation*. Thus, we find:

10   During this period of drought, the fire danger is rising.

where we understand *danger* as a mass noun that exists in perceptible quantities, and those quantities can be expressed in a vertical scale. In fact, the *amount* of anything is almost obligatorily expressed in vertical scale terms:

11   The temperature *peaked* at 104°.
12   These prices are *astronomical*

Even more abstract, and also more intriguing, are conceptual domains such as *argument*, which is understood as a kind of battle. What the authors showed was that when a mapping such as ARGUMENT IS WAR is invoked, all the trappings of *war* are available to talk about *argument*. Thus, one can *attack*, *defend*, *build* defensive perimeters, *cement* bricks in a wall or *retreat* in *constructing* an argument for or against something.

Similarly, our understanding of *time* crucially includes the fact that we view it as a valuable commodity, even as *money*. This leads to myriad expressions such as

13 You're *wasting* my time
14 We *invested* a lot of time in this new product
15 My car is living on *borrowed* time.

What is crucial about Lakoff and Johnson's claim is that metaphor is not a mere literary appendage, but rather is a crucial component of our understanding of and communication about the world around us, not only the physical, but, more importantly, the abstract conceptual and emotional world. As such, it pervades Language and serves as one of the most important motivations for extensions from the prototype to related meanings.

2.5 The Semantics of Grammatical Constructions

The final area in which Cognitive Linguistics analyses made their synchronic debuts was in fine-grained studies of the semantics of grammatical constructions that had traditionally been dealt with in standard Generative Grammar through transformations from identical (or similar) deep structures. For example, Langacker (1984), studied the classic transformational construction that had come to be known as tough-movement. Sentences such as

16 John is easy to please
17 Soda breads are easy to bake

were traditionally understood to be related to (in early Generative Grammar *derived from*) periphrastic sentences such as

18 It is easy to please John
19 It is easy to bake soda breads.[1]

A famous *New Yorker* article explaining Chomskyan linguistics and the generative semantics/interpretive semantics debate was entitled "John is easy to please", to reflect Chomsky's frequent use of the example of (16) in contrast with (20)

20 John is eager to please

to illustrate that there was structure 'beneath' the surface. Notably, *easy* is not predicated of *John* in anything like the way *eager* is predicated of *John*. And more importantly, *John* is understood as the 'object' of *please*, but not at all in (20), where *John* is, while not exactly the 'agent' of being eager, at least the experiencer, the person who is in the state of being eager. The various transformational analyses of these sentences accounted for that fact by making *John* the underlying object of *please* in (16), but subject of *please* in (20).

---

[1] In the earliest discussions of this kind of construction examples like (18) and (19) were understood to be 'underlying' and there was a transformation of 'it-replacement' (Burt 1971: 165), but later analyses involved either empty subjects or sentential subjects with the embedded subject moving 'up' to the matrix clause subject position and the remainder of the clause moving rightwards.

Langacker's task, then, was to account for these disparate constructions without the notion of 'underlying' anything, because it is a truism of Cognitive Linguistics that there is nothing beyond the actual utterances in the form that they appear in. Essentially, Cognitive Linguistics is a WYSIWYG ('what you see is what you get') theory.

He begins by noting that predicates such as *easy, tough, a cinch* etc. do not only occur in constructions like 17 (where one could reasonably conclude that their subjects were somehow 'inherited' from elsewhere, but also in cases like

21 Landscapes are tough [said to a beginning art student]
22 Hondas are easy [in a discussion of automobile repair]

Langacker argues that predicates like *tough* and *easy* are polysemous. They also involve a notion of *active zones*. Active zones involve, essentially, an abstract metonymy, where one aspect of a noun (or other entity) is invoked by use of another aspect. Consider, for example,

23 David blinked
24 I'm in the phone book

In (23), what 'blinked,' of course, are David's eyes, and what is in the phone book is my name and phone number. Although these are so unremarkable as to be unnoticed, Langacker argues that the same metonymy is being called on in (21) and (22); it's not *landscapes* that are hard, but painting them, and similarly for the ease of repair of Hondas.

Returning to *tough* and *easy*, he argues that their subjects are invoking active zones that are elaborated in their complements. Although both deal with (in this instance) a scale of difficulty/ease, one sense of *easy* takes a whole predicate as its trajector (figure, 'subject' in a semantic sense), while the other takes the object of the predicate that is the complement of the adjective (*to please* X). He diagrams these as follows (Figs. 2.4 and 2.5):

The diagrams are interpreted as follows. In the case of TOUGH, which is the sense illustrated in (22), the entire predication relates to a scale of *difficulty*, which is expressed by the vertical arrow. The level of normal difficulty is shown by the oval region labelled *n*. The landmark is in the region beyond normal difficulty, hence *tough*. The dark box represents some process with two participants, operating through conceived time (i.e. it is a process, rather than a state). The fact that the box itself is dark indicates that it *is* the trajector, that is, the thing being 'talked about', and it is located at the 'difficult' end of the difficulty scale.

For the diagram of the meaning of TOUGH, an example of the *easy to please* cases, the diagram is slightly different. While the process is still highlighted, it's now explicitly a transitive process (the energy flow, represented by the dotted downwards arrow, goes towards the inner highlighted circle), and the 'recipient' of the energy is the focused area within the active zone, marked as AZ, not as an actual trajector (in much the same way as John's eyes are what blinked, even when we say 'John blinked'). The actual trajector is the inner dark circle, and this would be filled out by 'Hondas' if they were 'tough to service'.

Fig. 2.4 Tough

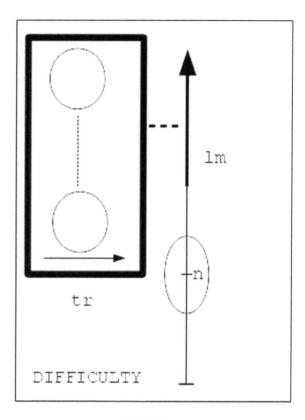

TOUGH

This finely detailed analysis exemplifies a major feature of Cognitive Linguistics, namely that constructions (and idioms, and almost everything else linguistic) are symbolic of meaning, and their meanings are built up out of parts that are themselves meaningful. As was stated above and will be elaborated in Chap. 3, the entire construction is *also* a linguistic unit, and, as such, may have meaning in addition to the meaning of the sum of its parts.

One additional example of fine detail, polysemy of meaning, and constructions having semantic content in addition to the compositional meaning of the units contributing to it, is found in Lakoff's (1987) discussion of the English Existential construction.

To begin with, recall that there has almost always been a 'there-insertion' transformation. The first example of its use is in Harris (1964: 196), and it can be found in most introductory Generative Syntax texts. Originally the idea was that any sentence with an indefinite NP subject and a BE copula (whether as a main verb or as an auxiliary) could be transformed into an 'existential' sentence by inserting THERE in place of the subject, moving the original NP after the BE, leaving the remainder to follow:

Fig. 2.5 Tough prime

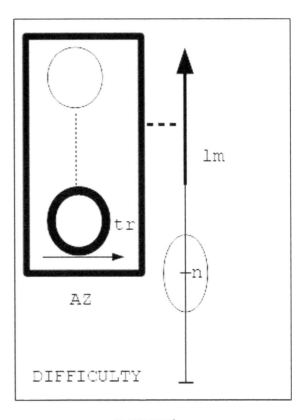

TOUGH′

25   A man was walking down the street →
26   There was a man walking down the street
27   A steam shovel is on the street →
28   There was a steam shovel on the street.

This analysis comes with all the standard generative assumptions: that there are meaningless morphemes (specifically *there*), that constructions that are related to each other do not necessarily differ in meaning (this was originally the whole idea behind 'deep structure', although that idea was abandoned in the seventies), and that the specifics of the existential construction were unrelated to whatever it means (assuming it actually has a meaning, which was usually not discussed, despite the fact that its name suggests a specific meaning).

   Lakoff begins by showing that rather than there being a sharp division between the purely deictic use of *there* in '*There's Joe!*' and the prototypical existential use: '*There's a reason for his bizarre behavior,*' there is instead a range of uses of *there* that suggest that the uses are instances of a single polysemous network rather than of two unrelated (or only historically-related) words.

Here are some examples of *there*, ranged along senses from purely deictic (visually present during the speech act, distal to the speaker and hearer) to the purely existential (*there* is totally non-deictic, meaning something like 'in reality, in existence'), or, finally, something like 'in the realm of discourse attention':

29 *There*'s the dog, behind the tree
30 *There* I was in the middle of the jungle
31 Now, *there*'s a great linguist![2]
32 *There* goes our last hope of winning this game.
33 *There* is a chance we'll win this game
34 *There* is no merit to his claim.
35 Once upon a time *there* were three bears.

Lakoff argues that the combination of meanings of the constituent parts add up, for the most common usage of this construction, to the introduction of a *new* item in a discourse context (the usage in 33), which is not only the prototypical instance of this construction, but also can explain some of the more curious restrictions on its use, such as the fact that it rarely occurs with definite noun phrases, and only in those cases when it is expressing a reminder:

36 Who else should we invite?
    There's the twins down the street.

Analyses such as these formed the basis of the initial appeal of Cognitive Linguistics to linguists unhappy with the generative program. The emerging theory offered motivated analyses of complex linguistic structures that accounted for all parts and the structures as a whole without the necessity of positing entities whose existence was justified solely on the grounds that the analyses needed them to come out right (such as the Complex NP constraint, later *subjacency*, still later other elaborate formal devices). Even the well-established 'movement' constraints of classical generative grammar turn out to have semantic explanations. Some analyses can be found in Deane (1992), while similar semantically-based analyses of pronominal use (Principles A, B, and C in generative grammar) can be found in van Hoek (1997); these are discussed in Chap. 5.

2.6 Early Diachronic Work

In addition to early synchronic explorations of Cognitive Linguistics of which examples are described above, the theory also attracted the interest of some historical linguists. The two studies described below were applications of the notion of a prototype-based semantic category to language change, first in the lexicon (Geeraerts 1988) and then in grammar (Winters 1989).

---

[2]Note that this example is actually ambiguous—it might be used at a cocktail party when someone spots Chomsky. But it also might be used in the non-literally-deictic sense evoked when people are, for example, discussing linguists they have met.

2.6.1   Lexical Change

In an early *Cognitive Linguistics* article, Dirk Geeraerts (1988) considered the notion of prototype (which had already evolved in some respect from Rosch's psychological work of the 1970s). He provides a case study of language change leading to a shift in prototypicality using the Dutch near synonyms *vernielen* and *vernietigen*, both meaning (roughly) 'to destroy'. They have different sources: *vernielen* attested in Middle Dutch and coming from the prefix *ver*, common to both verbs, and *niel* meaning, again roughly, 'down to the ground'; the verb, then, means 'to thrown down to the ground, to tear down'. The other verb is first attested in the 16th century, with *niet* (cognate to English *not*), giving rise to 'to cause to be nothing, to annihilate'.

Using the wide number of examples in the *Woordenboek der Nederlandsche Taal* (*Dictionary of the Dutch Language*), Geeraerts traces the development of both verbs, with emphasis on 19th-century usage. What is striking is that both the verbs, during that period, demonstrate the same range of meanings (both can indicate complete annihilation or something less than that which may still be called 'destruction'). They both are found with the same range of collocations as well, along a continuum from physical objects to abstractions and on to human beings. Where they differ is in the nature of the prototype and, hence, of the configuration of the extensions in these two polysemous semantic sets. The difference in prototype is further underlined by the fact that modern Dutch differentiates the verbs to a greater extent than was the case in the 19th century; the differing core meanings certainly contributed to the spread of contemporary usage of the two terms.

2.6.2   Grammatical Change

Geeraerts employed his description of the history of these two Dutch near synonyms as the basis for a discussion of the very notion of prototype. Winters (1989), on the other hand, took the emerging synchronic theory as more or less a given and used data on the history of the French subjunctive mode to explore ways in which semantic sets change over time. Fundamental to the analysis was the idea that each use was meaningful and indeed the 'meaning' of the subjunctive emerged from how it was used, either as an independent construct or in contrast to the indicative. Winters reviewed a series of uses of the subjunctive in Medieval French and proposed a semantic set for these uses, showing lines of extension from one to another. Her designation of a prototypical meaning arose from considering in general which of these meanings gave rise to others and, ultimately, which one meaning could account for all the immediate extensions from the core; that would be the prototype or best instance of the Old French subjunctive.

Once a semantic set for Old French was in place (provisionally at least), comparisons with later periods of French were possible. With these comparisons, changes within and across sets could be described. Some uses of the subjunctive disappeared completely (in indirect discourse, for example), while some became more or less prominent and others were added where the use of the indicative has given way to the subjunctive. What was particularly of note was that changes could take place under the influence of the prototype ('to hope' takes the subjunctive rather than the once universal future indicative in modern French in certain tenses, drawn in by a prototype expressing uncertainty in the outcome of what is being expressed in the subordinate clause). Other changes from one mood to another are motivated by semantically clearer peripheral uses: the conjunction use of 'before' implies that one cannot be sure of what happens next and has triggered the subjunctive since early French, while 'after', implying a greater degree of certainty, later become a trigger of the mood by analogy to 'before'. We must envision a period of overlapping usage/meaning to understand these changes.

To summarize, the data of mood at any period of French are complex and often messy. What Winters (1989 and subsequent revisions of the analysis; cf. Winters 1991, 2013), like Geeraerts, established in this early work was that Cognitive Linguistics could shed light on diachronic data and, ultimately, on the nature of language change. In doing so, these analyses and many subsequent ones called upon the same general cognitive functions as underlie synchronic language use.

2.7 Conclusion

As was seen in this chapter, early studies within the framework of Cognitive Linguistics were wide-ranging in their subject matter. Not only were they both synchronic and diachronic, but they quickly showed a multiplicity of approaches (compare the work on the semantics of so-called grammatical words and morphemes with the work on metaphor). The next chapter will address the theory as a whole as it exists now, followed by a chapter presenting a much wider range of case studies, triggered by the earliest work and subsequent expansions and revisions.

References

Brugman, C. 1981. *Story of over*. Bloomington: Indiana University Linguistics Club.

Brugman, C. 1988. *The story of 'over': Polysemy, semantics and the structure of the lexicon*. New York: Garland Press.

Burt, M.K. 1971. *From deep to surface structure: An introduction to transformational syntax*. New York: Harper and Rowe.

Chomsky, N. 1957. *Syntactic structures*. Janua linguarum. The Hague: Mouton.

Deane, P.D. 1992. *Grammar in mind and brain: Explorations in cognitive syntax. Cognitive linguistics research*. Berlin/New York: de Gruyter Mouton.

Geeraerts, D. 2010. *Theories of lexical semantics*. Oxford/New York: Oxford University Press.

Harris, Z. 1964. Co-occurrence and transformation in linguistic structure. In *The structure of language: Readings in the philosophy of language*, ed. J.A. Fodor and J.J. Katz, 155–210. Englewood Cliffs, NJ: Prentice-Hall.

Kuhn, T.S. 2012. *The structure of scientific revolutions* (with an introductory essay by I. Hacking). Chicago: The University of Chicago Press.

Lakoff, G. 1977. Linguistic gestalts. *CLS* 13: 236–287.

Lakoff, G. 1987. *Women, fire and dangerous things. What categories reveal about the mind.* Chicago: University of Chicago Press.

Lakoff, G., and M. Johnson. 1980. *Metaphors we live by.* Chicago: University of Chicago Press.

Langacker, R.W. 1979. Grammar as image. *Linguistic Notes from La Jolla* 6: 33–59.

Langacker, R.W. 1982. Space grammar, analyzability and the English passive. *Language* 58: 22–80.

Langacker, R.W. 1984. Active zones. *BLS*, 172–188.

Langacker, R.W. 1990. *Concept, image and symbol.* Berlin/New York: de Gruyter Mouton.

Langacker, R.W. 1991. *Foundations of cognitive grammar, Volume 2, Descriptive application.* Stanford: Stanford University Press.

Lindner, S.J. 1981. *A lexico-semantic analysis of English verb particle constructions with OUT and UP.* UC San Diego Dissertation.

Lindner, S.J. 1982. What goes up doesn't necessarily come down: The ins and outs of opposites. *CLS* 18: 305–323.

van Hoek, K. 1997. *Anaphora and conceptual structure.* Chicago: University of Chicago Press.

Winters, M.E. 1989. Diachronic prototype theory: On the evolution of the French subjunctive. *Linguistics* 27: 703–730.

Winters, M.E. 2013. Grammatical meaning and the old French subjunctive. In *Research on old French: The state of the art*, ed. D.L. Arteaga, 351–376. Dordrecht: Springer.

Chapter 3
Conceptual Underpinnings and Methodology

3.1 Introduction

The previous chapters provided a basis for a closer look at the theoretical frame-work of Cognitive Linguistics, first by considering its sources and secondly with an overview of some of the earliest synchronic and diachronic work which called itself "cognitive" in the sense set out in these early papers.[1] In this chapter we will extract theory from application, laying out both the basic commitments which were developed in the earliest explorations and those which have emerged in later work.

3.2 The Semantic Basis of Linguistic Structures

One of the strongest and most basic commitments of Cognitive Linguistics is that Lan-guage is symbolic of meaning. In some sense following Saussure (1974 [1916]), the argument is that all linguistic entities have only two 'poles', a semantic one and a phonological one. Langacker has stated this explicitly in all his work, from the earliest statements on Cognitive Linguistics. He says, for example "Lexicon and grammar form a continuum of symbolic elements. Like lexicon, grammar provides for the structuring and symbolization of conceptual content" (Langacker 1990: 12).

---

[1] During early 1991 there was a brief period of vigorous debate on the LINGUIST List, triggered by the call for participation in the second International Cognitive Linguistics Association conference, as to 'naming rights' around the term 'cognitive' with both the proponents of generative approaches and those of the then new theory rather fiercely defending its use. Over the following decades there has been a truce based on the general agreement that language use (production and perception) is largely a matter of cognition and that the disagreement resides in the way in which the human brain handles linguistic input. For the purposes of this volume we will, obviously, lay out the Cognitive Linguistics view with a short discussion of differences.

© The Author(s), under exclusive licence to Springer Nature Switzerland AG 2020   27
M. E. Winters and G. S. Nathan, *Cognitive Linguistics for Linguists*,
Expert Briefs, https://doi.org/10.1007/978-3-030-33604-2_3

For that reason, Cognitive Linguistics uses the cover-term of *unit* to refer to these entities—or elements—of all sizes. Further in that introductory chapter, Langacker says he conceives of the grammar as "providing the speaker with an inventory of symbolic resources" (Langacker 1990: 16). There are only three basic types of units, semantic, phonological, and symbolic. A symbolic unit is a unification of a semantic and phonological unit, but it is crucial to understand that "grammatical morphemes, categories, and constructions all take the form of symbolic units, and that nothing else is required for the description of grammatical structure" (Langacker 1990: 16).

This is, from the point of view of most contemporary linguistic theory, an extremely radical claim, because it posits that there are no meaningless elements in Language, neither morphemes nor words nor constructions. As such, this claim makes very specific requirements for any linguistic analysis. Every linguistic utterance must have semantic content (and, of course, formal, usually phonological, content as well—there can be no 'empty categories'). In short, both poles must have content.

By way of illustration, we will present some of the semantic primitives and concepts that have been used in many Cognitive Linguistics analyses of grammatical morphemes, lexical items, and constructions.

As we mentioned in the previous chapter, the semantics of linguistic units are normally presented in the form of *images*. 'Image' in Cognitive Linguistics' view refers to a structured representation of some domain, which can be physical (say, a room or a table), but also non-physical (say conceived time, or some aspect of motion, or some entity acting on some other entity, though, for example, containment or an implicational relationship). An important facet of this view of images is that the domain can be structured or *construed* in multiple ways. This may range simply from viewing a table from the top or from the side to viewing an action either from the viewpoint of the agent or the patient or even of the on-looker/speaker. Alternatively, it may view some action either as ongoing, or as having just been completed (it should be obvious that these latter notions are reflections of voice and aspect respectively). Through construal we arrive at conceptualizations as 'above' and 'below'

1 The shelf is above the desk.
2 The desk is under the shelf.

In (1) and (2) the objective placement of shelf and desk is the same, but the way in which this relationship is stated changes with the point of view of the speaker.

As was said in the previous chapter, a crucial aspect of the description of images is that some facet of the image is viewed as the *profile*, that is, the aspect of the image that the image is 'about'. The rest of the image is then the *base*. In many cases, a particular profile will only have meaning with respect to a particular base. For example, *uncle* is only meaningful within a kinship system, selecting a specific set of relationships from within a whole kinship network. Similarly, *point* (in the physical object sense only) assumes a base of which it is the 'point'. The choice of construal of the pair 'above' and 'below' will also serve to profile one or another of the objects in this relationship, be it physical (as in the desk and shelf just cited)

Fig. 3.1 Gone

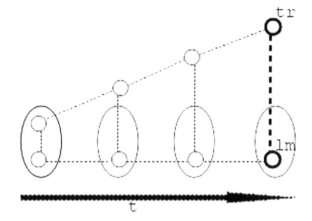

or lexically abstract (describing a university or industrial organizational chart may profile the CEO, 'above', or those reporting to her, 'below').

To examine an even more abstract grammatical example, taken from Langacker (1990: 6–7), consider the sentence.

3   When I arrived, he was already gone.

The overall image for *go* is of some entity (the trajector—tr) moving away from some other entity (the landmark—lm). The image for *gone* is a focus on the endpoint of such a process, and could be represented as in Fig. 3.1.

This is to be interpreted as follows. The arrow along the bottom represents a time-line, t (conceived time, of course). Each successive configuration from left to right shows increasing distance between two objects, of which one (the *trajector*) is conceived of as stationary, the other (the *landmark*) as moving. The darker combination of markings represents the *profile*, while the rest of the image is the base. Thus, the image profiles (essentially, focuses on) the endpoint of a process of movement.

The previous discussion illustrates the notion of construal as well as one of the sets of tools Cognitive linguists use to present semantic analyses. Other commitments should be mentioned. For example, one of the fundamental facts about the semantics of virtually every kind of unit in Language is polysemy. That is, it is the norm, rather than an exceptional case, that units have multiple meanings, and that these multiple meanings are systematically related to each other in motivated ways. Note too that the notion of semantics is a wide one, including what in other theories is often separated as 'semantics' and 'pragmatics'. Here all these considerations exist on a continuum of factors contributing to meaning; while core meaning, which is often the dictionary citation, will reside at the semantics end of this continuum (*telescope*, a device used to see objects at a distance), such considerations as the choice of French address pronouns (*tu* and *vous*) is also meaningful, though the meaning difference is more pragmatic than semantic. There is a vast middle section to this continuum where meaning is a mixture of the semantic and the pragmatic. This wide understanding of meaning arises in part from its polysemous nature; multiple meanings of a given unit arise from both its core and its usage.

Cognitive Linguistics makes no claim of linguistic universals, as opposed to cognitive universals like categorization. Rather, the substance of semantic categories is a function of the time in which language users live and the speech community (language or dialect) to which they belong. Finally, individual speakers construe meaning, both as produced and perceived, as a function of their circumstances, linguistic and other, at the time of the speech. Again, the act of construal is a universal, but the way in which construal leads to the assignment of meaning is a result of the individual or, through conventionalization, the speech community at a given time. In addition to the time and place specificity of many radial sets (see below), Cognitive Linguistics takes a certain amount of individual variation into account in proposing a semantic set.

Let us take a look at a simple example, taken from Geeraerts (2015), dealing with the English lexical item *fruit*. This word illustrates the complexity involved in specifying the meaning of a word, in that accounting for all of its senses includes a general understanding of its meaning as well as cultural knowledge, metaphor, and botany.

As we have seen, virtually all linguistic units have a prototype structure reflecting their semantics (we will address the nature of the phonological structure below in this chapter). *Fruit* is a good example. According to early work by Rosch (see, for example, Rosch 1975, 1977), apples, bananas, and oranges are prototypical fruit in western culture, while watermelon[2] and durian are not. Even worse instances would be coconuts. Of course, botanically, lemons and limes are closely related to oranges, yet neither are prototypical fruits. All of these instances are illustrations of how human categories are structured; to be a *fruit* you must be a seed-bearing 'pod' of a tree or plant that is not only sweet, but also treated as a dessert. Hence, we find the classic debate about tomatoes, which are seed-bearing but not sweet, and also do not usually figure in desserts.

But, of course, not all uses of *fruit* refer to edible objects served for dessert. Based on the concept that trees bear *fruit*, metaphorically other endeavors also bear *fruit*. Endeavors that do not bear fruit are therefore, *fruitless*, while those that succeed, are likely to be *fruitful*. In an additional, slightly archaic metaphoric use, children are the *fruit of the womb*. This term is actually a translation of a Hebrew metaphor (found in Psalm 127:3), probably entering wide use through the King James translation. Then, in a punnish playful extension, an underwear company named itself *fruit of the loom*, with an image of piled (literal) fruit as its logo. Interestingly, the fruit in the logo centers around an apple, with red, blue and (perhaps yellow) grapes surrounding a background of what appear to be grape leaves. The following figure maps visually the core of fruit and its extensions from the prototype (Fig. 3.2).

---

[2]We might argue about watermelon per se, but melons in general are not as prototypical examples of *fruit* as apples, bananas, and oranges, at least in much of American culture. The status of melons and other fruit types as prototypical or not depends in part on where one lives and when. But, even within a speech community, there can be differences.

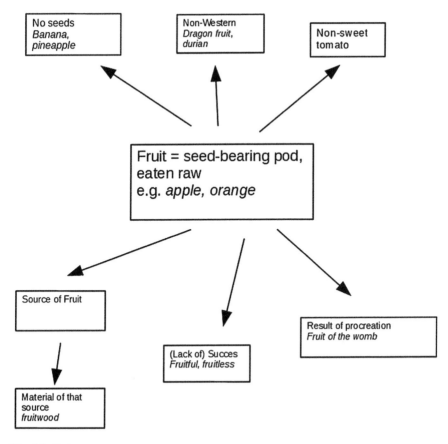

Fig. 3.2 Fruit

The hallmark of a radial prototype category, well illustrated by this word, is that there is no single set of *distinctive features* identifying members of the category. Rather there is usually a set of characteristics defining central members, but other members of the set can be related to the more central members through extensions such as change in perspective, abstraction, or metaphorical and metonymic extension. *Success* is only metaphorically a fruit, while *fruitwood* is wood from trees that bear fruit, a metonymic extension. The whole ensemble of category members belongs in the category for *motivated* reasons, but individual members may not necessarily share any distinctive feature with other members, other than that they can trace their justification for membership back to the same central prototype. It goes without saying that such a category is non-Aristotelian, in that there is no set of *necessary* and *sufficient* characteristics, but at the same time, it is crucial to note that membership in a category is not cognitively random. We cannot, for example, find a set of characteristics which unite children (*fruit of the womb*) and unsweet fruit (*tomatoes*) without understanding the prototypical meaning of this polysemous lexical unit.

Finally, in talking about category membership it is important to note that the metaphorical and metonymic extensions that account for disparate members of a category are *culture-specific* in many cases, as are, in cases like this one, the very core instances of the unit. Thus, there will almost certainly not be complete overlap between any linguistic unit in one language and a similar seeming unit in another. This, of course, accounts for the unreliability of translation of lexical items from one language to another. Although the prototypes may overlap (in obvious cases, such as *mother* or *hand*), the extensions will almost certainly not, and hence any particular use of one of these words in another language may or may not coincide with anything meaningful in another language.

3.2.1 Construction Grammar

A strand of linguistic research that began in parallel with Cognitive Linguistics, but has now partially merged with it is Construction Grammar. This theory received its impetus from Goldberg (1995), a seminal work that has sparked several research programs.

Construction Grammar dispenses with virtually all the apparatus of generative syntax, arguing that phrase structure and its rules are epiphenomena abstracted from much more concrete patterns consisting, to varying degrees of generality, of strings of words and word categories. Not only is syntax essentially linear, but Construction Grammar argues that the fundamental units, patterns of words and word classes, are themselves meaningful, and that each pattern, even if it were 'derived' from another in an old-fashioned transformational relationship in generative grammar, has an inherent meaning. As Goldberg (1995: 3) says:

> Differences in form [such as 'I am afraid to fall down' vs. 'I am afraid of falling down' and 'I loaded the truck with hay' vs. 'I loaded hay onto the truck'] led Bolinger (1968: 127) to conclude "a difference in syntactic form always spells a difference in meaning". The same hypothesis—which we may term the Principle of No Synonymy of Grammatical Forms—has been formulated by Givón (1985), Kirsner (1985), and Wierzbicka (1988).

Paraphrasing Goldberg, constructions are the basic units of Language. Patterns, normally consisting of slots and fillers, are constructions if something about their form or meaning is not strictly predictable from the properties of their component parts or from other constructions. Taking this view to its logical conclusion, even morphemes are constructions, in that they are pairings of meaning and form that are not predictable from anything else (Goldberg 1995: 4). Thus, in Construction Grammar, as in all versions of Cognitive Linguistics, no strict division is assumed between the lexicon and syntax. Lexical constructions and syntactic constructions differ in internal complexity, and also in the extent to which phonological form is specified, but both lexical and syntactic constructions are essentially the same type of declaratively represented data structure: both pair form with meaning (Goldberg 1995: 7).

As important is the understanding of a construction as being part of a network of constructions, and not part of an unstructured list. Rather, the network is interactive in that members at all levels (relatively subordinate or superordinate) can inherit features from each other; specific members may also override components of the basic construction. To cite an example used by Hoffman (2017: 313–314), the basic meaning of the ditransitive construction is the transfer of possession:

4 gave/sold She gives/sells/etc. the book to him.

With some members of the set, like *refuse*, the negative transfer overrides the potential for full ditransitivity:

5 She refuses (?him) the book.
6 *She refuses the book to him.

Frequency plays a role here for this version of Construction Grammar since the frequency of use of constructions is stored in the mental lexicon, that is, they become entrenched (Langacker 1987; Barlow and Kemmer 2000; Bybee 2013). The entrenchment may be either of the exact construction (form and lexical selection) or the same form with different complements (Goldberg 1995: 28):

7 She refuses him the book/answer/way out of his difficulty….

What is emphasized in this conception of grammar is the fluidity of the network. Nodes may inherit features from other members. The claim, of course, is that this kind of network mirrors cognitive functioning and, because of its interactive flexibility, accounts for linguistic creativity in a way that ties this creativity to the very nature of human linguistic processing.

In addition, related constructions are related to each other in the same way that we have seen other linguistic units related to each other through patterns of polysemy generated by extensions of metaphor, and the patterns may have prototypicality structures much like other units as discussed elsewhere in this book. For example, Goldberg (1995: 83) discusses the relationship between the caused motion construction:

8 Mary threw the ball into the crowd.

and the resultative construction:

9 The lava went from liquid into a solid within minutes.

as being a metaphorical change of location. That is, change is a metaphorical motion, and the end state is a metaphorical goal of that motion. So, constructions can have metaphorical extensions in the same way that lexical items can (as in 'This article sheds light on the problem'). A complex illustration of how constructions can be studied can be found in this chapter.

3.3   The Psychological Basis of Linguistic Structures

A second hallmark of Cognitive Linguistics is a very strong claim of psychological reality. The assertion here is not just that Language exists in the mind (as opposed to various abstract or even Platonic approaches), but that there are few if any language-specific functions, sometimes referred to as the 'language module' (Chomsky 1962). Rather, Language is produced and perceived by human beings using the same cognitive apparatus as for other ways of interacting with the surrounding universe (music or face recognition, for example).

A major way in which Language (again, at all levels of complexity) is processed and stored, for example, is through the fundamental cognitive function of *categorization*. As already mentioned and illustrated apropos of *fruit*, one kind of categorization is that organized around what cognitive psychologist Rosch (1978, 1983) has called the 'prototype' or 'best instance' of the category. Other related meanings exist in extensions from the prototype and may, in fact, not be related to each other unless this best instance is brought to bear.

Much has been written about prototype structures, both within Cognitive Linguistics and in the wider cognitive psychology realm (for a good summary see Murphy 2002), and further exemplification is not necessary here (see, for example, the discussion of *fruit* above).

Within cognitive psychology an additional view of categorization has emerged in the past few years, namely *exemplar theory*. Exemplar theory is crucially dependent on what has now become a standard view of human perception and memory, namely that humans remember and store enormous numbers of individual instances of perceptions (both objects and events). Many specific instances of birds, say, or apples are each stored, but, to the extent that they are similar to each other, are stored near each other (in a metaphorical spatial sense, of course). As Baayen and Ramscar (2015: 106) describe the process, "exemplar models start from the assumption that learners acquire and store an extensive inventory of instances of language use (…exemplars) in memory. Instead of seeking to account for the productivity of language through abstract rules operating over hand-tailored representations, exemplar models base their predictions about novel forms on these stored exemplars, in combination with a general, domain aspecific similarity-driven algorithm".

Exemplar theory counters the general generative view that storage is expensive, computation is cheap, with the contrary view, that storage is cheap, and computation can be minimized. There is extensive evidence that speakers store a great deal of information about individual speech instances, including such information as the identity of the speaker and even the physical location and emotional state of the hearer.

There is more to the psychology of language than concept formation (or even what concepts are in the first place). A great deal of recent Cognitive Linguistics research has focused on how learning takes place, and, in particular, on what has come to be called the 'quantitative turn' (Janda 2017). There are several reasons for this development. One is the view that Cognitive Linguistics is a usage-based model of linguistic structure. It posits no "fundamental distinction between 'performance' and 'competence', and recognize[s] all linguistic units as arising from usage events. Usage events are observable, and therefore can be collected, measured and analyzed scientifically" (Janda 2017: 500).

This view translates into a general methodology for the study of language acquisition. "Usage-based, constructivist approaches assume that children acquire linguistic knowledge from the language that they hear. Linguistic knowledge is represented in the form of constructions, which can be thought of as form-function pairings (again, harkening back to Langacker's formal and semantic poles), and rather than using rules to produce new utterances, children are assumed to operate by analogy" (de Ruiter and Theakston 2017: 59). It is believed that "children are building functionally or semantically motivated networks of words based on their distributional co-occurrences. The slot in a construction is seen as a generalization over all the items that appear in that position, and is a function of both the number of items appearing in that slot (type frequency) and their semantic heterogeneity" (de Ruiter and Theakston 2017: 62). There is considerable evidence that children are highly sensitive to frequency, not only of words but also of constructions. For example, de Ruiter and Theakston report that "in multiword utterances, [younger] children are more accurate in repeating high- than low-frequency four-word phrases even when the frequency of the individual components is closely matched… Also, three- and four-year-olds make fewer errors (e.g. uninversion errors like *Why she is hitting?) in wh-questions if the question begins with a high-frequency wh-word + auxiliary-verb combination" (de Ruiter and Theakston 2017: 65). Such results are incomprehensible if learning is strictly rule-based as frequency of occurrence of constructions should not affect the frequency or ease of access of the individual items contained therein.

While frequency is part of the story, there are other considerations as well as to language acquisition and language change. Also in play is the notion of salience, a factor in the assignment of parts of a unit to the profile or the landmark. What is salient stands out, precisely through the ways in which it is being profiled, where the ways may include intonation and phrase or sentence stress, word order, and even word choice. This profiling may be cultural as well; although cranes are not indigenous to Japan, they play an important cultural role and Japanese speakers will pick the crane out as a best instance of the category *bird* without ever having seen one.

Langacker (1987: 59–60) suggested that the effect of repetition of salient items is their becoming entrenched in the brain (he surmises that neurological pathways will one day be mapped onto these high frequency units). Much of what a child acquires early are such conventionalized items. On the other hand, novelty plays a part as well. New meanings arise as well, from figurative usage, most often metaphoric or metonymic. Such playing with language (if we may state it this way) leads to new meanings, again in this widely semantic way which incorporates pragmatic variation as well. It is here that lack of frequency is most important; novelty is another source of salience, contradictory as it may seem (Keller 1985 considers frequency and novelty in the framework of the 'invisible hand'). These somewhat countervailing phenomena both play a role, then, both in child language acquisition and adult language change.

3.4   Conceptual Blending

An additional semantic tool that was added in the late nineteen nineties was the concept of *conceptual blending*. The definitive statement can be found in Fauconnier and Turner (2002), although other work preceded it. Blending is distinct from metaphor, in that two roughly equal domains are blended together, leading to novel conceptualizations that flow from the blend, rather than one domain being understood through the lens of another (a simplified way of thinking of metaphors).

One clear instance of a novel blend that has become so ingrained that we are unaware that it is a blend is the notion of 'desktop' in a computer (as seen in Windows and the Macintosh screens) (Fauconnier and Turner 2002: 22–23). The blend takes as one domain a literal desktop, with a flat surface on which physical objects can be rearranged, along with folders, pens, and drawers. The other domain is, of course, computer programs and data storage, which, at the time the blend was invented, consisted of magnetic storage on a physical disk, in an essentially linear fashion (this method of storage, a mechanical hard drive, still exists, but has been supplanted in many cases by solid-state storage on such objects as usb drives and phones and tablets).

The blend consists of treating certain sets of data as being in *files*, which are stored in *folders*. The folders can be moved around on the desktop (exactly as cardboard folders can—note that the onscreen icon *is* of a cardboard folder). The folders have labels, although not every feature in one domain is necessarily selected for use in the blend—for example, the label isn't on the tab on a desktop. On the other hand, another blend, that of folders in a desk drawer, is used to arrange multiple pages in a web browser. That blend retains the labels on the tab.

Of course, much of the blend is novel as well. For example, while we can drag literal folders, we normally just lift them up. And we open electronic folders by double-clicking on them, since they are, to the extent they exist at all, two-dimensional. Yet, as Fauconnier and Turner point out, this blend was so easy to understand and manipulate that it instantly took over virtually all computer operations, and has continued onto mobile device adaptations such as phones and tablets.

Another instance of a blend discussed in depth in Fauconnier and Turner comes from an entirely different domain. They cite a print ad for an 'education excellence' program that shows three preteen children in an operating room wearing surgical scrubs. The headlined caption reads "Joey, Katie and Todd will be performing your bypass". The blend is of eight-year-olds who might be taking advanced science classes, and you, some time in the future, needing a bypass, and hoping that you will have competent surgeons. The reasoning is of course that you will support special science education in grade schools so that these children can be trusted to perform your bypass. As the authors say "the ad is powerful because it uses blending brilliantly to bring together children as they are now with the frames they will inhabit much later on. The reader is also projected into the blend, as the patient. This makes a distant situation urgent by bringing it into the immediate present" (Fauconnier and Turner 2002: 66).

Blends have become an important tool in semantic and pragmatic analyses. For example, Turner (2015: 228–229) cites Nikiforidou's analysis of the use of the word *now* in past tense narratives as blending the author's viewpoint while telling the story with the protagonist's viewpoint when some past event was taking place ('Once refrigeration was invented it was *now* possible to ship perishable items long distances').

3.5 Methodology

Early work in Cognitive Linguistics, under the influence of the prevalent methodology of the period, called upon speaker intuition (and most often that of the linguist her/himself) as the primary approach to illustrating and confirming theoretical statements. Some of that work is laid out here in Chap. 2 (Langacker 1982; Lakoff 1987) and some below in Chap. 4 (Achard 2007, Winters 1987). While such data may be plentiful, they are chosen to support some point being made; there are certainly no claims as to their being experimentally grounded, complete, or even extensive. Almost from the beginning of interest in this approach to Language, however, practitioners were challenged as to the validity of their use of introspection to support claims of mental activity. We will look at two methods here, first experimental evidence and secondly corpus studies and the application of big data to language analysis.

3.5.1 *Experimental Evidence*

Gibbs (1996: 33ff and references therein) points to lab-based work whose goal was to address the question of whether all meanings of ambiguous (polysemous) items are activated as part of comprehension (a modular, autonomous view) or whether the same results are indicative of non-autonomous processing. While the results are inconclusive if the intention is to uphold or refute modularity, when viewed within the framework of Cognitive Linguistics (that is, along with a view of pervasive polysemy, among other commitments), they are suggestive of non-modularity. Other comparatively early psycholinguistic work by Gibbs (reported in Gibbs 1996: 44–49) tests human processing of metaphors and, with these results, supports the pervasiveness of metaphor beyond literary figures.

More recent work studies metaphoric conceptualization (Gijssels and Casasanto 2017) looking at the interaction between two domains by testing through experimentation the notion that people use space to talk about time because they use space to think about time. The authors (p. 651) emphasize the deeper understanding of cognitive activity that can be achieved in testing this relationship; they are not simply confirming linguistic analysis. In short, they find that the same metaphors do not necessarily occur in thought as in language, in particular in terms of the orientation they use to conceptualize and verbalize time through space (horizontal as opposed to vertical) and the number of dimensions which enter into the metaphors (one as opposed to three).

3.5.2 Corpus-Based Synchronic Studies

Cognitive Linguistics, like other frameworks, has benefitted from what is now called big data, available through the compilation of large corpora and the technology supporting sophisticated mining. Gries (2010) provides a discussion of how such studies might be carried out, based on the underlying notion that differences in meaning correlate with differences in the distribution of a given lexical item or larger construction. Earlier studies (cited p. 324) usually limited themselves to base forms, and only looked at two-dimensional comparisons. Gries, however, has developed more sophisticated analytic tools which allow for wider studies. He illustrates this with the very polysemous English verb *run* showing how a multidimensional analysis can account for prototypical meanings ('fast pedestrian motion') and allow for those involving path, source, and goal:

10   He ran down the street/from the fire/to the shelter.

Other differences are subtler, but appear robustly in data sets and can be better accounted for where context can be flagged as well. They are among the many extensions of *run*, analyzable as a set around the prototype of rapid pedestrian motion.

11   They were so in love, they thought only of running away.
12   He was so abusive, she thought only of running away.

Gries demonstrates the development of finer-grained studies supported by big data within the cognitive framework, linking them to wider use of corpora, but also showing the affinity for these analyses for exemplar and usage-based frameworks.

3.5.3 Corpus-Based Diachronic Studies

Corpus mining techniques have been applied as well in diachronic studies. In a paper presented in 2017, Klaus Hofmann looks at a relatively recent development of the subjunctive in English. Using the *Corpus of Historical American English*, which collects data from 1860 to 2000 for fiction and non-fiction including journalistic texts, he sampled instances of subordinate clauses triggered by the verbs *ask*, *demand*, *insist*, *order*, *recommend*, and *suggest* with the goal of noting subjunctive (or non-subjunctive) use. The first four of these verbs are more or less canonical as triggers of the subjunctive, since they are direct orders, while the last two are more indirect and are more likely than the first group to trigger a modal (primarily *should*) rather than a subjunctive. Examples with the subjunctive with both kinds of triggers include the following in decreasing order of directness of the command for action:

13   He demanded that Livingston call him. (1993)
14   I must ask that you keep my secret safe. (1993)
15   … someone did suggest she call a private detective… (2015)

What Hofmann found was that the use of the mood in these less prototypical
contexts (called the 'mandative' use since it contains an indirect request for action
on the part of another person) has increased over the course of the 19th and 20th
century to the point where its frequency is greater than for the more canonical uses.
Where in the first period (1860–1900) *ask* was a trigger of the subjunctive more
often than *suggest* which tended to be found in conjunction with a modal expression,
suggest becomes more usual with the subjunctive in the second period (1900–1930)
and is now (data from 1930–2000) as frequent or more so.

The explanatory analysis calls upon prototype theory, with the shifting of the prototype from more direct triggers to less direct ones over time. The reason, Hofmann
continues, is a dual identification, first of the bare verb in the subjunctive with the
bare verb after a modal (*that he be, that he should be*) and secondly of the meaning
of the subordinate clause which, schematically, calls for the action of one person
as a result of a speech act uttered by another. The explanation is both formal and
functional, then, but with the form of the base verb stemming from one or another
mandate, either direct or indirect, and thus broadly semantic of itself.

3.6   Conclusion

With this chapter we have set out the various facets of Cognitive Linguistics which
define the theory and differentiate it from other current approaches to Language.
There are two important points. The first is that Language is, first and foremost,
meaningful and that meaning is polysemous; not only do morphemes and so-called
content words (nominals and verbals) have a complex semantic basis, as they are also
viewed in many theories. Rather, all units of whatever size are meaningful. This has
resulted in the exploration of the meaning of what have been called 'grammatical'
words, notably prepositions and adverbs. At the other end of the scale, Cognitive
Linguistics holds that meaning is the basis for syntax; grammatical structures of
all sizes (phrases, clauses, sentences) are constructed based on the meaning each
element conveys. Units of this size may also be polysemous by their nature, and all
meaning is understood as encompassing what in other theories is divided between
semantics and pragmatics. Not only do units take their interpretation by the place
and time in which they are being used, but also according to the way the unit is being
construed within a larger structure.

The second major element of Cognitive Linguistics is its very strong claim as
to psychological reality. Again, differing from other theories, it rejects the notion
of specifically linguistic mental structures; human beings, rather, produce and per-
ceive Language using the same functions (assignment of salience and categorization,

among others) that we use for other mental activity like music or face recognition and processing.

The next chapter will provide illustrations, drawn from synchronic and diachronic studies of both word and construction meaning. It will also introduce, though case studies, the ways in which Cognitive Linguistics has been applied to the least meaningful of linguistic units, phonemes and sounds.

References

Achard, M. 2007. Complementation. In *Handbook of cognitive linguistics*, ed. D. Geeraerts and H. Cuyckens, 782–802. Oxford/New York: Oxford University Press.

Baayen, R.H., and M. Ramscar. 2015. Abstraction, storage and naive discriminative learning. In *Handbook of cognitive linguistics*, ed. E. Dąbrowska and E. Divjak, 100–119. Berlin/Boston: de Gruyter Mouton.

Barlow, M., and S. Kemmer (eds.). 2000. *Usage-based models of language*. Cambridge, UK: Cambridge University Press.

Bolinger, D.L. 1968. Entailment and the meaning of structures. *Glossa* 2: 119–127.

Bybee, J.L. 2013. Usage-based theory and exemplar representations of constructions. In *The Oxford handbook of construction grammar*, ed. T. Hoffman and G. Trousdale, 49–69. Oxford/New York: Oxford University Press.

Chomsky, N. 1962. Explanatory models in linguistics. In *Logic, methodology and philosophy of science*, ed. E. Nagel, et al., 528–550. Stanford: Stanford University Press.

Fauconnier, G., and M. Turner. 2002. *The way we think: Conceptual blending and the mind's hidden complexity*. New York: Basic Books.

Geeraerts, D. 2015. Lexical semantics. In *Handbook of cognitive linguistics*, ed. E. Dąbrowska and D. Divjak, 273–295. Berlin/Boston: de Gruyter Mouton.

Gibbs, R. 1996. What's cognitive about cognitive linguistics. In *Cognitive linguistics in the redwoods: The expansion of a new paradigm in linguistics*, ed. E.H. Casad, 27–53. Berlin/New York: de Gruyter Mouton.

Gijssels, T., and D. Casasanto. 2017. Conceptualizing time in terms of space: Experimental evidence. In *The Cambridge handbook of cognitive linguistics*, ed. B. Dancygier, 651–668. Cambridge, UK: Cambridge University Press.

Givón, T. 1985. Function, structure and language acquisition. *The cross-linguistic study of language acquisition, Volume 2*, 1005–1028. Hillsdale, N.J.: Lawrence Erlbaum.

Goldberg, A.E. 1995. *Constructions: A construction grammar approach to argument structure. Cognitive theory of language and culture*. Chicago: University of Chicago Press.

Gries, S.T. 2010. Behavioral profiles. A fine-grained and quantitative approach in corpus-based lexical semantics. *The Mental Lexicon, 5*(3), 323–346.

Hoffman, T. 2017. Construction grammars. In *The Cambridge handbook of cognitive linguistics*, ed. B. Dancygier, 310–329. Cambridge, UK: Cambridge University Press.

Janda, L. 2017. The quantitative turn. In *The Cambridge handbook of cognitive linguistics*, ed. B. Dancygier, 498–514. Cambridge, UK: Cambridge University Press.

Kirsner, R.S. 1985. Iconicity and grammatical meaning. *Iconicity in syntax*, 249–270. Amsterdam/Philadelphia: Benjamins.

Lakoff, G. 1987. *Women, fire and dangerous things. What categories reveal about the mind*. Chicago: University of Chicago Press.

Langacker, R.W. 1982. Space grammar, analyzability and the English passive. *Language* 58: 22–80.

Langacker, R.W. 1987. *Foundations of cognitive grammar, Volume 1 Theoretical prerequisites*. Stanford: Stanford University Press.

Langacker, R.W. 1990. *Concept, image, and symbol: The cognitive basis of grammar. Cognitive linguistics research 1*. Berlin/New York: de Gruyter Mouton.

Murphy, G.L. 2002. *The big book of concepts*. Cambridge, MA: MIT Press.

Rosch, E. 1975. Cognitive representations of semantic categories. *Journal of Experimental Psychology: General* 104: 192–233.

Rosch, E. 1977. Human categorization. In *Advances in cross-cultural psychology*, ed. N. Warren, *Volume 1*. London: Academic Press.

Rosch, E. 1978. Principles of categorization. In *Cognition and categorization,* ed. E. Rosch and B. B. Lloyd, 27–48. Hillsdale, NJ: Lawrence Erlbaum.

Rosch, E. 1983. Prototype classification and logical classification. In *New trends in cognitive representation: Challenges to Piaget's theory*, ed. E. Skolnick, 73–86. Hillsdale, NJ: Lawrence Erlbaum.

de Ruiter, L., and A.I. Theakston. 2017. First language acquisition. In *The Cambridge handbook of cognitive linguistics*, ed. B. Dancygier, 59–72. Cambridge, UK: Cambridge University Press.

Saussure, F.D. 1974 (1916). *Course de linguistique générale. Edition critique préparée par Tullio de Mauro*. Paris: Payot.

Turner, M. 2015. Blending in language and communication. In *Handbook of cognitive linguistics*, ed. E. Dąbrowska and D. Divjak, 211–232. Berlin/New York: de Gruyter Mouton.

Wierzbicka, A. 1988. *The semantics of grammar*. Amsterdam/Philadelphia: Benjamins.

Winters, M.E. 1987. Innovations in French negation: A cognitive grammar account. *Diachronica* 4 (1–2): 27–53.

Chapter 4
Case Studies

4.1 Introduction

The previous chapter laid out the basic theoretical elements of Cognitive Linguistics, with an emphasis on its semanticity. The theory, to review, makes strong claims of psychological reality of a specific kind, and stemming from these views of mental structure, provides various insights into the very nature of language production and perception. Language users categorize linguistic units in much the same way they categorize other aspects of their physical and interior worlds, assigning membership to what are called radial sets arranged around the best instance or prototypical example of the unit. Units are, with very few exceptions, polysemous, hence the complex structure of a great many of these semantic sets. Finally, since all Language is essentially meaningful, Cognitive Linguistics is based on a continuum of these meaningful units, ranging from bound morphemes through words and compounds to syntactic units, both simple and complex.

Pervasive themes through all the case studies in this chapter include the semanticity of all linguistic units and the polysemy of the great majority of them. First, pervasive semantic content can be briefly illustrated by Langacker's discussion (1991: 265, based on part of Chap. 4 of Bolinger 1977) of the so-called meteorological *it* ('it is raining', French 'il pleut', German 'es regnet'). Through an argument that will not be detailed here, Langacker demonstrates that *it* is indeed meaningful; we are not dealing with an empty morpheme (a contradictory term within Cognitive Linguistics), but rather one with a special kind of meaningfulness.

Secondly, let us look a little more closely at the notion of polysemy. Chapter 2 contains a discussion of Lakoff's (1987) analysis of *there*, like meteorological *it*, a so-called expletive morpheme. It will not be repeated here except to emphasize the fact that even something as abstract as *there* or *it* is not only meaningful, but may have more than one meaning. What is important is that there may be many degrees of abstraction in the use of a given unit and some may range from quite concrete to quite abstract (see the section on French *pas* below in this chapter).

Finally, by way of an introduction, one of the consequences is that the traditional line between semantics and pragmatics has been, at the least, made fuzzy. There are clearly semantic units at one end of this continuum (*book* and some other concrete nouns are examples) and clearly pragmatic ones at the other end (the meaning of personal address pronouns in languages with more than one). A large number of units, however, lie somewhere in the middle where the distinction between semantic and pragmatic meaning or use is neither clear nor useful.

4.1.1 Chapter Outline

The rest of this chapter will look at a variety of case studies, examples of Cognitive Linguistic analyses. The next section deals with syntactic matters, both synchronic and diachronic, while Sect. 4.3 briefly addresses morphology and the lexicon. Synchronic approaches have been largely set out in Chaps. 2 and 3, so the emphasis here will be on diachrony. Finally, Sect. 4.4 will look at how phonology can also be subsumed within this theory, using the same approach and taking advantage of the same mental structures as this framework employs for meaningful units. Again, as with other linguistic components, the discussion will be both synchronic and diachronic.

4.2 Syntax

4.2.1 Synchronic Studies

Some early studies have already been considered in Chap. 2, Langacker (1984) on subject raising and (1987) on the passive, as well as Lakoff (1987) on existential *there*. Because Generative/Transformational Grammar was the (almost) unchallenged mainstream theory in the 1980s and 1990s, much syntactic work within the Cognitive Linguistics framework was intended to demonstrate that the same phenomena could be accounted for using a semantics-based approach. We will look briefly at two more of these analyses, followed by a recent rather traditional study and end this section with another, related syntactic framework.

4.2.1.1 Generative/Transformational Constructs

In *Anaphora and Conceptual Structure* (1997), van Hoek provides an alternative analysis to what in the Chomskyan model was called c-command, the identification of a series of constraints capturing the relationship of nominals to each other in a clause or sentence. Typical pairs of sentences illustrating the phenomenon are the following, where in each case the pronoun and noun are coreferential[1]:

---

[1]The following discussion of c-command is based on van Hoek (1997: 2ff).

1 Near her$_i$, Elaine$_i$ spotted the house.
2 *Near Elaine$_i$, she$_i$ spotted the house.
3 Elaine$_i$ loves her$_i$ mother.
4 *She$_i$ loves Elaine's$_i$ mother.

Using the notion of c-command, Reinhart (1983 and in a series of papers) described the play of grammaticality and ungrammaticality by stating that the first nominal (NP1) c-commands the second, and hence renders the relationship grammatical, if and only if neither NP dominates the other directly and if the first branching dominating NP1 also dominates NP2, that is, if they both descend from the same higher node. In the following tree, B c-commands C, D, and E, while C can only command B, and D and E command each other:

5

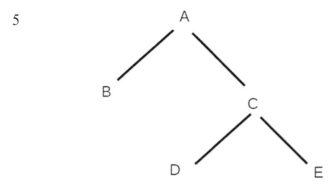

The description is successful in that it can provide a list, like the one here, of the grammatical and ungrammatical relationships between nominals. What it does not do, van Hoek continues, is explain why this is so.

Her proposal is based on the notion of a scale of accessibility or salience, where full noun phrases rank low since all information about their referentiality is provided and pronouns rank high since they must generally be understood through some sort of co-reference. This scale is semantic rather than structural, since it refers to a world outside of the clause itself; that much is obvious. For the rest, van Hoek makes use of the idea of domain (cf. Langacker 1987) to delineate the scope of reference. As she points out (p. 5), the advantages of this approach include the smaller number of theoretical constructs needed (simply the accessibility scale as opposed to tree structure and the various clauses of c-command). In addition—and, we would say, crucially—the same notion of accessibility is valid not only at the clause level but across clauses and even more widely in discourse. What we have is an analysis falling at the pragmatic end of the semantics/pragmatics continuum, elucidating how language users track participants.

Deane (1991), like van Hoek, undertakes cognitive reanalysis of the syntactic phenomenon of island constraints famously addressed by Ross (1967) within the framework of Transformational/Generative Grammar. The earlier work found a syntactic solution to the lack of grammaticality of sentences like the following, where the first is the declarative underlying the ungrammatical question:

6   You know the man that X saw.
        *Who do you know the man that saw? (Complex Noun Phrase Constraint)
7   You talked to Bill and X.
        *Who did you talk to Bill and? (Coordinate Structure Constraint)
8   For you to meet X is easy.
        *Who is for you to meet easy? (Sentential Subject Constraint)

In all these cases the ungrammaticality stems from the inability of English syntax to allow long-distance extraction to form an interrogative from certain kinds of complex structures, in (6) from a subordinate clause, (7) from a coordinate expression, and in (8) from a complex subject. Ross loosely unified his account for these somewhat disparate structures under the heading of 'island constraints', claiming that certain kinds of structures were like islands, totally surrounded by water and therefore not to be left by walking away. As part of the broader generative enterprise, he claimed that their existence substantiated the autonomy of syntax; there was no semantic reason for these kinds of sentences to be ungrammatical and they should be thought of as purely syntactic exceptions to more general rules.

Deane (1992), working within Cognitive Linguistics, looked instead for semantics-based explanations which link these phenomena to general cognitive structures, where semantics must be thought of as what Geeraerts (2010) calls "maximal", not confined to dictionary meaning alone (p. 14). Deane first points out that the numerous exceptions to these constraints are evidence that we are dealing with something which cannot be captured by an autonomous syntax. One can examine, for example, the framing of individual verbs with contrasting grammaticality (p. 11, his example (21)); in all these cases, the corresponding declarative sentence ('I sought/appreciated/described' etc.) are grammatical:

9   Which posts did you seek/refuse an appointment to?
10   ?Which posts did you appreciate/discuss an appointment to?
11   *Which posts did you describe/study an appointment to?

Deane calls upon various cognitive functions like that of domain, also used by van Hoek, as well as the spreading of activation of attention in the brain, applied here to grammatical structures, but, as a conceptualization, applicable to many sorts of non-linguistic attention. He points (p. 18ff), for example, to the varying relationships between verbs and the nominals attached to them, at varying degrees of closeness and makes the claim that grammaticality is a matter of degree of the activation of one by the other. It is here, too, that he makes use of Lakoff's (1987) work on metaphor and metonymy, among other pathways between verbs and nominals. Where the relationship becomes sufficiently tenuous, grammaticality judgments fail, both through hesitation and outright rejection, where rejection can signify an inability to understand what is being said. Deane's goal, as was said above, was to establish the non-autonomy of syntax using these data, but he does so not just by confirming their variability and openness to exceptions (even Ross (1967) had already pointed this out), but by showing a broadly semantic, cognitive pathway to a more unified description and explanation of island phenomena.

4.2.1.2   The Standard Approach

The studies accounting for existential *there* (Lakoff 1987) and for the English passive
(Langacker 1987) set the stage for a multitude of analyses using the same theoretical
apparatus, or, to be clear, theoretical approaches based on each of these pioneers.
Lakoff (1987) laid out the radial set (see Chap. 3 here for a full discussion) and
used the complex data of *there* to demonstrate the potential for wide application
of the semantic category organized around a prototype. As was also discussed, his
interest is not just in the nodes of a semantic set, but also in the lines which connect
them; metaphor and metonymy play a large role in how meanings, including the
meaning of grammatical structures, are related one to another. Langacker's approach
(1987 and many papers since) has been to emphasize the ways in which mental
conceptualizations of time and space function in Language. To simplify by way of
illustration, a nominal expression, therefore, is a bounded (spatial) area not primarily
thought of in relationship to time, while a verbal expression is generally bounded
primarily through its temporal conception.

Achard (2007) has continued these well-established ways of approaching syntax as meaningful. His subject is complementation, viewed cross-linguistically and
across types ranging from full clauses (those with a tensed verb) to infinitives. In
line with Givón's (1980 and subsequently) binding hierarchy, Achard demonstrates
that in English, French, and Japanese the choice of complement type reflects the
broad meaning of the governing verb, where part of the meaning is the degree of
governance the verb has over its complement. The less involved the subject of that
verb is in the complement, the more complex the complement itself, so that (12) is
a verb of cognition, (13) expresses desires vis-a-vis someone else, and (14) desires
about oneself.

12 He knew she left.
13 I want her to leave.
14 I want to leave.

The correlation of these broad semantic types and their complements cross-
linguistically is striking even taking language-specific variation into account. In
French, for example, where the subjunctive is far more employed than in English,
the hierarchy remains the same despite this difference; (15), (16), and (17) are trans-
lations of the immediately preceding English examples:

15 Il savait qu'elle était partie. [indicative]
16 Je veux qu'elle parte. [subjunctive]
17 Je veux partir. [infinitive]

Again, verbs of knowing take full, indicative complement clauses, verbs of desire
take the subjunctive complement (a full clause, unlike the English, but marked by a
change in mood), and verbs of personal desire are followed by the infinitive.

Achard goes further in that he also includes the so-called 'raising' and 'equi'
verbs and their complements:

18   Mary seems to understand.
19   Mary wants to understand.
20   It seems that Mary understands.

While (18) and (19) look similar, their structures are quite different in that in (19) Mary is indeed the subject of *want* and *understand* but in (18) Mary is only in some sense the subject of *understand*—that is, she is not *doing* the *seeming*. Transformational accounts used the notion of 'raising'; *Mary* moves from the lower clause to the higher one to become the apparent subject of *seem*. If, however, one thinks of Langacker's notion of active zones (1987: 485), then within that zone *Mary*, through the relationship with *understand*, is more than an apparent subject (although not an agent) and the need for a syntactic mechanism like raising is obviated. Achard also, importantly, calls on the notion of construal to differentiate (18) from (20); we are considering the same event from two viewer perspectives where one emphasizes Mary as understanding and the other the likelihood, but not certainty, of this understanding. We have discussed time and place specificity in Chap. 3; Cognitive Linguistics also sets forth speaker specificity, not just in the traditional sense of idiolect, although that is important, but also as a point of view relative to a specific situation which shapes the way that situation is conceived of and expressed.

4.2.2   Diachronic Studies

4.2.2.1   Grammaticalization

Cognitive Linguistics has, from the 1980s, also been applied to diachronic matters (Geeraerts 1986; Winters 1989; Sweetser 1990). Many of the early studies as well as those being carried out today make reference to the semantic set and, in some basic ways, explore how the set can change over time, with regard both to what sets may exist at any point in time and also how they are configured. Winters (1992) provides a typology of such changes. A summary of the development of negation from Latin to French (Winters 1989) will illustrate some of the ways in which language change can be explained through this theoretical apparatus.

The data are as follows, using one short sentence with the same meaning throughout: in Latin the standard mode of verb phrase and sentence negation was through the use of the particle *non*.

21   Non amat.
      NEG love 3 person sg.
      She does not love.

In old French, *non* has become *ne*, and often stands alone before the verb.

22   Ele ne aim.

A variation, however, is the use of a further particle *mie* or *pas* normally (but not always) following the verb.

23 Ele ne aim mie/pas.

Eventually *mie* becomes obsolete and *pas* becomes an obligatory part of a discontinuous negation; this is the formal standard today (24). A less formal variation (25), occurring mostly in spoken French, drops the pre-verbal segment *ne*, with *pas* as the obligatory marker of negation:

24 Elle n'aime pas.
25 Elle aime pas.

   The key point in this brief diachronic story is the development of the post-verbal negative segment. Both *mie* and *pas* come from Latin, *mie* from *mica* 'crumb' and *pas* from *passus* 'step', respectively, the smallest amount one can eat and the smallest distance one can move. One can surmise that, like many other designators of least amounts, they were used first for emphasis ('She didn't even eat a crumb', 'He didn't walk a single step') and later became fixed as negative polarity items, much like Modern English *soul* in expressions like 'She didn't see a soul she knew'; the non-polarized form still remains (although modern French emphasizes the smallness of 'crumb' by adding a diminutive to form *miette*), but with the literal meaning, while the polarized meaning is closer to 'not at all'. What is most interesting is that these polarity items expanded their scope so that in attested Old French, when we find them (they are variable in use), they coexist with any verb at all, appropriate or not to ingestion or to movement. We have already noted the disappearance of *mie*, but must note as well that it was a general negator, actually used more frequently than *pas* before it fell out of use.
   A second key point is made in examples (24) and (25). With the disappearance of *ne* in most oral French and in less formal writing, *pas* has become the sole negator. Semantically it seems completely separated from the non-polarized meaning 'step' as evidenced by the fact that standard dictionaries use two different entries for the two units. We have also found that linguistically naive speakers of French are surprised (and charmed!) by the historical connection between them. Fig. 4.1 summarizes what has been said above here.
   Cognitive Linguistics, therefore, can be applied diachronically as well as synchronically. The story of *pas* is one, first, of the development of new meanings (the emphatic which in turn becomes the polarity item, and, ultimately, the prototypical negator), which for some time remain in the same semantic set. Ultimately, however, *pas* 'step' separates from *pas* negator after a period of overlap as a polarity item. We would argue that this is a model for a great number of cases of grammaticalization, the evolution of a full unit (noun, adverb, preposition, etc.) into a grammatical marker of some kind. In the case of *pas*, the phonological pole remains intact, where in others (Romance adverbial marker *-ment/mente/miente* from Latin *mens/mentis* 'mind') it becomes a clitic and, in this case in modern French/Italian/Spanish, a fully attached ending.

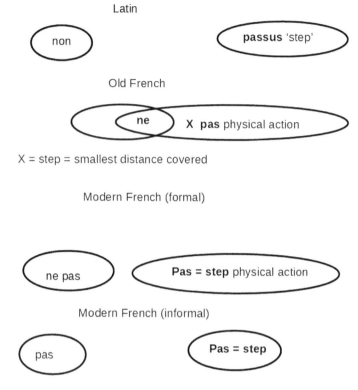

Fig. 4.1 French negation

4.3 Morphology and the Lexicon

4.3.1 Synchronic Studies

Chapter 3 contains several examples of ways in which lexical items and morphemes have been analyzed in this framework. It is important to emphasize that the line between them is not a sharp one; all meaningful units are on a continuum of size and complexity. It is also the case that perceived levels of complexity can be misleading; to continue with the examples in the earlier chapter, *fruit* is certainly a complex category, but so are some which have not been thoroughly considered in the past and usually dismissed as meaningless, including prepositions (*out, over*) and grammatical morphemes like the past participle.

Each of these units, when analyzed within the cognitive framework, can be captured by a radial category centered on the most prototypical instances and containing various extensions which may or may not be relatable to each other if one does not take the prototype into consideration. A further example, not to be expanded on here in great detail is *cup*; the term is used in American English for the equivalent in weight of two sticks of butter, each a quarter of a pound (there are 16 oz. in a pound) and also for sports victories (winning the Stanley Cup in hockey[2]). It is difficult to associate these directly, especially since neither necessitates a physical cup, but the use of the same lexical item must be understood via a physical prototype of a certain size, material, and use.

Of equal importance, then, are the lines of extension from the prototype, as we illustrated with metaphors in previous chapters. As was said, these serve an explanatory purpose; they show how language users can move from one use to another of a given unit since the associations exist in the mind. If they are repeated often enough, they become cognitively entrenched, paths of relationships which are therefore conventional, at a given time in a given dialect.

Kay and Fillmore (1999: 1) is an extended example of how Construction Grammars deal with the complexity of syntactic structures without the need for phrase structure rules or movement metaphors. In arguing against the need for phrase structure rules they say: "This means that the relatively general patterns of the language, such as the one licensing the ordering of a finite auxiliary verb before its subject in English [in a simple interrogative sentence], and the more idiomatic patterns, such as [*[to] have to hand it to [someone]*] stand on an equal footing as data for which the grammar must provide an account."

As might be guessed from the title of the article, it deals with the exclamatory construction roughly abbreviated 'What's X doing Y?'. Kay and Fillmore make a strong argument that this construction is a unified linguistic unit, despite the fact that it has open slots, some of which can be filled by several kinds of constituents, and spans two clauses, thus making it impossible to describe with a finite state phrase structure grammar. In particular, it has a conveyed meaning in all of its instances, namely an exclamation of incongruity at the situation being described. Here are a number of instances, illustrating the variability in the slot-fillers as well as the overall meaning (Kay and Fillmore 1999: 24):

26a. What is this sociologist doing *in my living room*? (locative prepositional phrase)
  b. What is that kid doing *with my shoes on*? (absolutive prepositional phrase)
  c. What are you doing *without any shoes on*? (absolutive prepositional phrase [negative])
  d. What are you doing *with all that money*? (with meaning 'having')
  e. What are you doing *without the money*? (*without* meaning 'not having')
  f. What is it doing *raining on my birthday*? (verb: present participle)
  g. What is she doing *covered with mud*? (verb: passive participle [stative])
  h. What are you doing *naked*? (adjective)
  i. What is she doing *the winner*? (noun)

---

[2]It does involve a physical cup, but the term has been extended to refer to the victory itself, probably more frequently than to the cup as an object.

It is important to note that this is a *construction* with a specified meaning (roughly incredulity at something anomalous). Paraphrases immediately revoke the pragmatic sense and invoke the literal (non-idiomatic) sense, or else become ambiguous. Consider, for example, 26b. If we remove the adverbial *on*, leaving

27 What is that kid doing with my shoes?

it can mean *either* surprise that the kid is wearing my shoes, or an actual inquiry about the activity the kid is engaging in. Many of these are actually ambiguous between literal and incredulity senses, or can be easily modified to acquire the additional sense.

4.3.2 Diachronic Studies

The semantic set also captures language change, as was clear from the syntactic examples above. There can be changes in the prototype itself or in various of the branches extending from it; a new extension would be an expansion of the set, while others may disappear or become more or less prototypical. Other changes occur when units within a set become, by addition or substitution, part of other sets which in themselves may already exist or be created by this change. Finally, we should consider what Lakoff (1987) and Johnson (1987) converge in calling 'image schema transformations', as will be discussed below.

4.3.2.1 Changes Within and Across Sets

It is, however, difficult to compartmentalize these changes, despite this logic of possible modifications, since many changes combine movement both within and across sets. The grammaticalization of *pas* as a general negator in French is one such. It begins as an extension of the basic Latin meaning 'step', but eventually moves to another set where it has lost its motion sense and retains only negation. While direct proof is hard to find, the fact that there are two entries for 'step' and negator in standard French monolingual dictionaries is a clue to how the units are perceived. A slogan for a brand of shoes carries another hint: *pas un pas sans Bata* ('**not** a **step** without Bata') would not be catchy without the pun on the two quite distinct meanings of *pas*.

   On the lexical level, change in units can be quite complex as well. The development of English *book* is such a case. It is generally accepted that it is a cognate of *beech*, a northern European tree (cf. OED, s.v. *book* where various objections to this source have been cited and, to a great extent, refuted). The first link is to the use of wooden writing tablets, presumably made of beech wood, and hence what is written on these tablets. We have an extension of the prototypical tree meaning, therefore, via a metonymy to material derived from the tree and hence to the content recorded on this material.

It is with the movement from the material (beech wood) to the content that we have a split, with the *written* meaning becoming the center of a new set. It remains the center through multiple changes in material (clearly no longer the salient prototypical indicator of a *book*) from wood to vellum and then to paper. While this physical object continues to be central in the understanding of the unit, another transformation takes place, from the physical to the mental: *book* becomes the content rather than the object. It is at this point that *writing a book* can occur in any medium (the current one is being typed on a computer); one can talk of a book in progress before anything is recorded at all and reading a book is increasingly an electronic process involving no paper at all.

4.3.2.2 Changes in Prototypes

Identifying the prototype and thus its evolution is not necessarily straightforward at all times, as has been discussed elsewhere. With *book*, this is certainly the case, especially since the development of technology allows for increasingly metonymic uses of the word for non-physical units which, nonetheless are readable, the prototypical use of the basic unit. We would surmise that the prototype is still the physical object (people talk of going to the library for 'real' books and about how they prefer the touch and even smell of paper), but it is certainly in competition with the notion of *book* content, both mental ('parts of this book are still only in my head') and technological ('I just downloaded a great cookbook and want to try some recipes'). Although we will not pursue this here, note also that there are other extensions of the word that, while originally motivated by the 'bound volume' sense have moved quite far from the prototype. We are thinking here, for example, of the verb extension *book a flight, book tickets to a show*, as well as to *book it*, meaning to move quickly.

Grammaticalization will provide some clearer cut examples of prototype shift. One can, roughly, divide the outcomes of this complex of changes into two: either the full word continues to exist or it does not. In the case of French negation, the two meanings of *pas* remain, although native speakers do not seem to be aware of their shared history unless they have been given explicit information about it. This is also the case for the Romance future, where reflexes of the verb 'to have' have developed into much reduced personal endings. They are morphologically distinct in some persons and at least look like the full forms with the meaning of 'possession' in others. There is a split into two semantic categories involved, each with its own prototype, but not the movement to a new prototype within the set.

Loss, or at least partial loss, of the source category in grammaticalization can be illustrated by a cross-linguistic phenomenon in the development of spatial adverbs and prepositions. In many instances they come from body part names, an unsurprising path given the role of embodiment in human construction of meaning (Johnson 1987). Some are transparent: *alongside (of), facing, at the foot of*. The nouns *side, face,* and *foot* make up part of the expression in ways which allow speakers to see the connection and, we would surmise, maintain a single semantic set with the adverbial/prepositional use as an extension, albeit a distant one. Others are less clear; *behind* is still found in the expression *hind quarters*, but used only for animals. The prototype has shifted, and the animal use is peripheral. Finally, there are some where the connection is completely lost; *in front of* or *fronting* have no current body-part reflex (it relates to French *front* 'forehead') and are clearly central in a purely adverbial/prepositional set. Similar ranges of association pertain in languages as diverse as French and Hebrew.

4.3.2.3   Image Schema Transformations

Both Lakoff (1987) and Johnson (1987) define image schemas as overarching cognitive constructs, based on schematic notions such as *over* and *in*, embodied notions of the human place in the world relative to other human and non-human entities. Chapter 2 provided examples of our ability to transform these image schemas so that *over*, although prototypically designating a superior position, can also be used in rotation to cover something from below (papering *over* a hole in the ceiling, for example). It can also be transformed from a static location to path ('She lives over the hill' to 'We walked over the hill'). Consider as well the transformations from a container to the content of the container (a *cup* of coffee, to the *coffee* itself—*I drank three cups*), to the content even when no container is present (a *cup* of butter as measured by the number of sticks of butter in American packaging).

   In all these cases, the transformation may be viewed as synchronic or diachronic; following Sweetser (1990) we can assume that the most closely physical of the relationships are the earliest to be developed, with transformations following chronologically. In some, in fact, there may be competing prototypes, so that, in addition to *over* as a physical relationship (the oldest of the uses), a second usage viewed as prototypical may be the more recent one of *over* in the sense of 'complete' (*the play is over at 10:30*).

4.4   Phonology

One of the merits of Cognitive Linguistics is that it can account for units of all sizes using the same human cognitive apparatus. When it comes to phonology, however, there are added factors since underlying it is the phonetic reality of sounds. This is not to say that phonology is simply formalized phonetics, but that the human vocal apparatus and human auditory ability both impose some limits on what sounds are possible, both in isolation and in combination. Resulting from those limitations are more abstract phenomena; the notion of what is the 'same' sound. These physical constraints, however, do not make it impossible to talk about a cognitive phonology, but rather add certain kinds of nuances not found in the lexicon or in most of grammar, although one parallel might be the limitation on human memory required for the production and perception of multiply embedded sentences.

4.4.1 Synchronic Studies

In a series of papers, Nathan (1986, 1989, 1995, 1999, 2015) explored the nature of the phoneme within the framework of Cognitive Linguistics. Like work in grammar and the lexicon, this approach is based in categorization and, more specifically, the nature of the radial set. Like other units, phonemes are categories with a prototypical member and other members derived by lines of extension from the central, or best, instance. It is in defining these lines of extension that articulatory and auditory factors take on importance, as the following examples, one vocalic, followed by a more complex consonantal set, will illustrate.

4.4.1.1 French /e/

Contemporary standard French, as spoken in France, has a single front mid phonemic vowel /e/. It has two phonetic manifestations, [e] and [ɛ]. The higher [e] appears in open syllables and the lower [ɛ] in closed. We can argue that the higher vowel is the prototypical one on several grounds: first, it is the name of the sound, pronounced [e]. Secondly, because of the nature of French, there are more open syllables than closed, not just as a matter of historical accident, but because all intervocalic consonants are pronounced with the following vowel, rendering all syllables followed by a single consonant open. In a syllable-timed language like French, this elision is a prominent feature. Finally, there are, indeed, more open syllables with [e] as their vowel, in part because many of the most common irregular verbs show an [e] in the first person singular (arguably the most frequent of forms): *j'ai* 'I have', *je fais* 'I do', *je vais* 'I go'. The last form also functions as a future marker. In addition, commonly used past tenses have [e] as their ending: the imperfect for all but the first and second person plural (*j'allais* 'I was going', etc.) and the majority of past participles found in the compound past in all persons (Fig. 4.2).

For all these reasons, we can propose /e/ as the prototype with a single line of extension from it to the conditioned allophone. One might argue that we have done nothing more than reschematize the structuralist approach of phoneme and allophone, with the one distinction that the primary allophone (the higher variant /e/) is also the prototype, and functions to observers (and linguists) as the label for the phoneme. This is certainly true in the sense that the phonological facts are the same, but by using a radial set, one can see how lines of extension can be explanatory; here each one is motivated by the nature of the syllable, ending in a vowel or a consonant. As we have already said, phonology is different from other components of Language in that it involves human vocal and auditory physiology, but these physical features play a role similar to that of metaphor or metonymy in serving to create extensions from

Fig. 4.2 French /e/

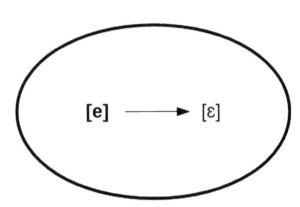

/ e /

the prototype; It is beyond the scope of this book to motivate the auditory/acoustic reasons for the higher allophone being the prototype, or for the connection between the lower vowel and closed syllables. The following example will demonstrate further ways in which this approach to phonology unites it with other linguistic components.

4.4.1.2 English /t/

Further information about the nature of the phonological set can be gleaned from contemporary English /t/. As Fig. 4.3 shows, it has four extensions, [t], [tʰ], [ʔ], [ɾ], united in one set by the fact that they are all perceived as /t/ by native speakers and all spelled with the letter t̪. The first and second of these, [t] and [tʰ] are the most common, the former, the unaspirated reflex, appearing after an initial [s] and the second, the aspirated variety. The third, [ʔ], appears in syllable- or word-final position before other consonants (*batman, sit down!*) and the fourth, [ɾ] in American English intervocalically following a stressed syllable (*lighter, shut up!*).

The question of how the prototype is determined is more complex here than with French /e/, just above. It is the case that aspirated [tʰ] is the most frequently appearing reflex of /t/. It is also the one cited by native speakers in isolation whether or not they would aspirate the same sound in context ("What is the sound at the beginning of *top*? After the 's' of *stop*?"). This fact leads one to argue that it is the version speakers are most conscious of; certainly that eliminates [ʔ] and [ɾ] which are quite certainly produced at a subconscious level.[3] There exists, however, one argument for [t] as prototypical; it is, as pronounced, the reflex with fewer features than the [tʰ].

---

[3]One exception is due to a dialect difference: American English speakers flap /t/ intervocalically while most dialects of British English do not. In imitating (or trying to imitate) British speech, American speakers will make of a point of saying [pɪti] and not [pɪɾi] as a salient marker of the

Fig. 4.3 English /t/   /tʰ/

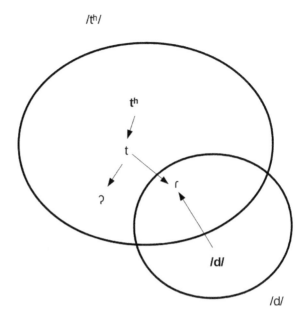

Since choice is necessary for this figure, we have made [tʰ] the prototype, but the arguments here are intended to underline the complexity of the choice even where the set itself is relatively straightforward.

Another point about phonological categories is that there may be overlap, as there is in semantic categories. As is well known, the reflex [ɾ] is not only a part of the /t/ set, but also of the voiced /d/. What is captured here is the neutralization of voicing of the alveolar obstruent in intervocalic position, leading to mishearings in some contexts of *writer* as *rider* and vice versa.

One final point here is that Nathan identified the extensions of allophones from the prototype, in general motivated by phonetic considerations, as being the articulatory equivalent of image schema transformations. In fact, because the modification of, say, a voiceless alveolar stop to a voiced flap also occurs in mental speech, it is not only the equivalent of an image schema transformation; it actually *is* one.

4.4.1.3 Synchronic Conclusion

In summary, the approach to phonology through the framework of Cognitive Linguistics serves several purposes. It is capable of grasping the various phonological processes present in Language, often through the overlapping of phonological sets; the confusion of /d/ and /t/, for example. It is important to note that the phonological sets are not just another notational method, but rather an explanatory claim as

---

difference. It is also the case that American speakers *sometimes* hear the flap as 'sounding like' a /d/. Interestingly, and relevant here, is that they never hear a 'real' /d/ as sounding like a /t/.

to what occurs during the production and perception of speech. Finally, again, its value lies in its parallelism to the ways in which other components of Language are produced and perceived, although always with the caveat that the human articulatory and auditory apparatus play a role here in ways that they do not on the semantic side of Language. This is not to say that meanings cannot be reanalyzed because of phonological overlaps, but that reanalysis would have a phonological component as well.

4.4.2   Diachronic Approaches

As with other components of Language, phonological change over time can be described and explained using the apparatus of Cognitive Grammar. The first part of this section will be a general consideration of types of sound changes and the second will be a closer look at Latin /l/ and its development in the Romance languages.

4.4.2.1   General Phenomena

The synchronic examples above emphasized the configuration of the phonological set, a phoneme and its variant pronunciations, some allophones in the structuralist sense and some not entirely so. These sets can also be viewed as dynamic across time, illustrating the effects of contiguous segments which lead to mergers of phonemes and to splits either within the set or across sets.

The French phonemic vowel /e/ is the result of the merger of two phonemes, /e/ and /ɛ/. Unusually for sound change, this one occurred and has become fully audible in living memory in the same geographic area; there are, however, still speakers who are influenced by spelling and pronounce final -ais/ait/aient of the imperfect and conditional tenses with /ɛ/ rather than /e/. These speakers are, on the whole, older and more conservative in their speech; younger speakers and those with less conservative pronunciation have merged the sound with /e/, with the results described above.

Other kinds of change can also be captured through dynamic aspects of phonemic sets; we can look at them using the rather well-known data of the Germanic series of changes summed up under the label of umlaut.[4] The Old High German plural marker in certain noun classes was a high front /i/; a non-syllabic version of the same sound (/j/) was also the marker for diminutives. Through the phonetic process of anticipatory assimilation, a back vowel in the noun stem became front, although still rounded, contrastively apparent today in the plural and diminutive:

---

[4]The description of umlaut as presented here is simplified; it is being used to illustrate what the Structuralists called primary and secondary split. The notation used to specify the change has no theoretical status—it's simply an abbreviation.

28 [back] > [-back] / _____ X [-back]

When the stem vowel was /u/ or /o/, the result was a new front rounded vowel, /y/ or /ø/ respectively. When the stem vowel was /a/, the newly fronted vowel also raised to /ɛ/, a preexisting sound. Simply by way of illustration, examples would be the plural of Modern German *Gast* [gast] 'guest', the plural of which is Gäste [gɛstə] 'guests'.

Let us take this last vowel change first. The result is not a new phonemic set, since /ɛ/ was already part of the phonemic inventory, but simply the addition of a variant, based on a new environment for [ɛ], at least as long as the following /i/ remained. Once it disappears, either by being deleted or merging with other vowels as a schwa, the set of /ɛ/ has, phonetically, fewer extensions. However, spelling may play a role in the development of this phonological set; the sound [ɛ] is spelled with an e in most cases, but the outcome of umlaut is rather spelled ä, with the diaeresis marking the fronting of a previously back vowel. In highly literate societies like those where German is spoken, one could argue for at least some level of consciousness of two kinds of /ɛ/ based on spelling, although the sounds are fully merged.

The two higher vowels provide a different kind of case: in each instance speakers of German have created totally new sounds. They are phonetic variants at first, [y] as an extension from long [u] and [ø] of long [o] in the presence of a following [i]. Once the conditioning element disappears, the new sounds are, of course, not predictable, and split from /u/ and /o/ respectively as full phonological sets of their own. In these cases, spelling is a reminder of origin again, since the sounds are rendered as ü and ö. Figures 4.4 and 4.5 summarize these changes.

Where there are three phonemes in the long back vowel series in Old High German, each with two extensions, modern German has added a new front rounded series at the high and mid levels; among the low vowels, we have a merger. In all cases the spelling of the sounds coming from the former conditioning element may suggest, given the literacy of most speakers, that there is still some cognitive awareness of two different 'kinds' of [ɛ].

4.4.2.2 /l/

One last case study will emphasize the overlapping of phonological sets and their subsequent separation. For it we will use Old French /l/ or at least the variants for which we have evidence.[5] The phonological set had three variants, based on spelling and on subsequent changes: [l], [ɫ], and [ʎ]. The palatalized variant, [ʎ] is marked by spelling (variously il, ille); there is no spelling evidence for the other two varieties, but we can surmise that there were both a clear and dark /l/ based on later phonological events. The Old French phonetically conditioned variants ([ɫ] before a consonant or at the end of a word, [ʎ] before a palatal, with [l] elsewhere) continue to change,

---

[5]There will be no discussion of devoicing of [l] in the vicinity of a voiceless consonant, as in *oncle*; we have no evidence for older versions of the language since there is no orthographic indication of this variation any more than there is currently. A full study of French /l/, synchronically and diachronically, would have to take it into account as part of extensions of the phonological set.

Fig. 4.4 Old high German
Umlaut

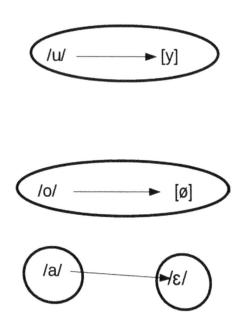

Old High German Umlaut

through contact with other phonological sets. This contact, or overlapping occurs because of phonetic changes in the extensions of [l]: [ʎ] and [ɫ] both lose laterality and merge, respectively, with [j] and [w]). Here again, spelling, in its conservatism, may affect the mental category.

Figure 4.6 shows the period of overlap of phonemes, with the subsequent full movement of what had started as palatalized and velarized [l] to other sets.

4.4.3   Conclusions

Phonological units at first seem like outliers in the context of Cognitive Linguistics since one cannot claim a semantic pole for them. It is the case, however, that it is possible to conceive of the configuration of the phonological set as sharing many features with the semantic set: the phoneme itself is equivalent to the prototypical member, with the understanding that the phoneme is also a pronounceable sound, while variants (allophones and other modifications) of the prototypical member are the same as extensions in semantic sets. The principle difference is in the lines of extension. Rather than metaphors, metonymies, and image schema transformations,

Fig. 4.5 Later German Umlaut

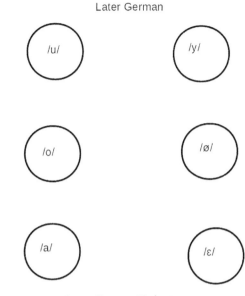

Fig. 4.6 French /l/

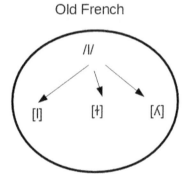

the extensions are often phonetic, hence articulatory or auditory in nature, and, as explained earlier, can be thought of as phonetically-motivated image schema transformations.

Once phonological sets can be established, they can be studied as well across time. New extensions may arise through phonetic conditioning of various kinds. They may remain members of the original set, merge with other sets, or even break off completely to form new sets. These possible changes correspond to the development of new conditioned or unconditioned allophones, the complete merger of phonemes, or the split of sets, either through the loss of some extension to another set or through the development of a new set. What Cognitive Linguistics has to offer is that when looked at—both synchronically and diachronically—through its lens, one can better understand how phonology makes use of the same cognitive functionality as do meaningful units. We compare sounds to prototypical examples and, as a result, use categorization as our way of producing meaningful utterances and also understanding, on a phonetic level, what is said to us.

4.5   Chapter Conclusions

This entire chapter consists of examples of the application of Cognitive Linguistics, in syntax, morphology and the lexicon, and in phonology. In each of these linguistic subcomponents, both synchronic and diachronic examples have been provided. For all but phonology, the theory posits a continuum of complexity across meaningful units, using to do so a broad definition of meaning which includes what in other theories may be divided between pragmatics and semantics. There is a recognition here that there are degrees of semanticity and pragmatic content, but holds that the difference is one of degree, not of kind.

Change, therefore, is change in meaning, where meaning is expressed in radial categories organized around prototypical members and extensions. The configuration of extensions may change over time, as may the conceptual notion of what is the prototypical instance of the set. Sets may split from each other and may merge as well. The causality of change is, of course, complex. Its spread, as argued widely, depends crucially on frequency of use, both among adults and children at the acquisition stage. Various theories of actuation bring into play the prevalence of metaphor, metonymy, and the transformation of image schemas, often through novel expressions, to arrive at something novel (though not too novel) which, if salient enough to catch the attention of users (either in larger or smaller groups), may spread and be incorporated as part of conventionalized language.

Phonology concerns itself with units without inherent meaning. As has been demonstrated, the configuration of phonological units mirrors the configuration of prototype-based semantic sets. This is the case synchronically as well as diachronically where sets are modified along the same lines as sets of meaningful units. The major differences lie in the lines of extension and of change among members of the units and across sets; the motivation is physiological and/or acoustic, that is, concerning both human articulation and the ways in which sounds are heard and interpreted.

References

Achard, M. 2007. Complementation. In *Handbook of cognitive linguistics*, ed. D. Geeraerts and H. Cuyckens, 782–802. Oxford/New York: Oxford University Press.

Bolinger, D. 1977. *Meaning and form (English language series, no. 11)*. London/New York: Longman.

Deane, P.D. 1991. Limits to attention: A cognitive theory of island constraints. *Cognitive Linguistics* 2 (1): 1–63.

Deane, P.D. 1992. *Grammar in mind and brain: Explorations in cognitive syntax (Cognitive linguistics research)*. Berlin/New York: de Gruyter Mouton.

Geeraerts, D. 1986. Functional explanations in diachronic semantics. *Belgian Journal of Linguistics* 1: 67–93.

Geeraerts, D. 2010. *Theories of lexical semantics*. Oxford/New York: Oxford University Press.

Givón, T. 1980. The binding hierarchy and the typology of complements. *Studies in Language* 4 (3): 333–377.

Johnson, M. 1987. *The body in the mind*. Chicago: University of Chicago Press.

Kay, P., and C.J. Fillmore. 1999. Linguistic generalizations: The what's X doing Y? Construction. *Language* 75 (1): 1–33.

Lakoff, G. 1987. *Women, fire and dangerous things. What categories reveal about the mind*. Chicago: University of Chicago Press.

Langacker, R.W. 1984. Active zones. In *BLS* 10: 172–188. Berkeley: Berkeley Linguistic Society.

Langacker, R.W. 1987. *Foundations of cognitive grammar, Volume 1, Theoretical prerequisites*. Stanford: Stanford University Press.

Langacker, R.W. 1991. *Foundations of cognitive grammar, Volume 2, Descriptive application*. Stanford: Stanford University Press.

Nathan, G.S. 1986. Phonemes as mental categories. *BLS* 12: 212–224.

Nathan, G.S. 1989. Preliminaries to a theory of phonological substance: The substance of sonority. In *Linguistic categorization, Amsterdam studies in the theory and history of linguistic science. Series IV, Volume 61,* Current issues in linguistic theory, ed. R. Corrigan, F. Eckman, and M. Noonan, 55–68. Amsterdam/Philadelphia: Benjamins.

Nathan, G.S. 1995. How the phoneme inventory gets its shape-cognitive grammar's view of phonological systems. *Rivista di Linguistica* 6 (2): 275–288.

Nathan, G.S. 1999. What functionalists can learn from formalists in phonology. In *Proceedings of the symposium on formalism and functionalism*, ed. M. Darnell et al., 305–327. Amsterdam/Philadelphia: Benjamins.

Nathan, G.S. 2015. Phonology. In *Handbook of cognitive linguistics*, ed. E. Dąbrowska and D. Divjak, 253–273. Berlin/New York: de Gruyter Mouton.

Reinhart, T. 1983. *Anaphora and semantic interpretation*. London: Croom Helm.

Ross, J.R.R. 1967. *Constraints on variables in syntax*. Dissertation, MIT.

Sweetser, E.E. 1990. *From etymology to pragmatics*. Cambridge, UK: Cambridge University Press.

van Hoek, K. 1997. *Anaphora and conceptual structure*. Chicago: University of Chicago Press.

Winters, M.E. 1989. Diachronic prototype theory: On the evolution of the French subjunctive. *Linguistics* 27: 703–730.

Winters, M.E. 1992. Schemas and prototypes: Remarks on syntax change. In *Diachrony within synchrony: Language history and cognition (Duisburger Arbeiten Zur Sprach- und Kulturwissenschaft) 14*, ed. G. Kellermann and M.D. Morrissey, 265–280. Pieterlen/Bern: Peter Lang.

Chapter 5
Expansions and Newer Directions

5.1 Introduction

Cognitive Linguistics has not remained static over the decades since it emerged. As can be seen by the examples in the last chapter, its scope expanded rather quickly to all aspects of core linguistics, both synchronic and diachronic. As such, it has continued to grow. It has, however, also expanded in other new directions which have not only addressed acquisition and sociolinguistic topics within the general field of linguistics, but have built connections with literary theory as well, generally through metaphor. What is most striking, as will be seen in this chapter, is that the notion of a usage-based model continues, with some exceptions (also to be discussed) to point Cognitive Linguistics toward further unification as a full theory of Language.

5.2 Cognitive Insights

5.2.1 Usage-Based Models

Although the earliest developments in Cognitive Linguistics were heavily semantic/pragmatic in nature, or dealt with what kind of categories linguistic units belonged to (such as radial prototypes, and exemplar models), suggestions early in Langacker's work (1988) spurred a parallel thrust to take extremely seriously the view that there are no language-specific learning mechanisms, and that all information about linguistic structures that serves as input to the 'language acquisition device' must be contained in the linguistic input itself. In short, there is no 'language acquisition device', and human beings have no special *linguistic* faculties that are distinct from all other kinds of learning. This means that all language acquisition must be based solely on the linguistic data available to the learner. On the other hand, as most psychologists now believe, humans are capable of remembering enormous numbers of specific linguistic events (conversations, sentences, words) in very great detail

© The Author(s), under exclusive licence to Springer Nature Switzerland AG 2020   65
M. E. Winters and G. S. Nathan, *Cognitive Linguistics for Linguists*,
Expert Briefs, https://doi.org/10.1007/978-3-030-33604-2_5

(including such information as the speaker's identity, the circumstances surrounding the utterance, perhaps even the emotional state of both the speaker and the hearer). These 'data' then serve as the input to general processes of schematization and abstraction that result in what we call the 'grammar' of the language.

Learners, therefore, have access to multiple instances of sentences, constructions, words, and even individual sounds, out of which they must construct a grammar. However, there is no necessity that the grammar be a set of abstract rules. Rather a grammar is a structured set of more or less abstract patterns, based on the afore-mentioned 'data', some of which are quite general (roughly equivalent to the old generative formula S —> NP + VP), while others may be as specific as the idiomatic expression *X is the new Y*. There is no limit to the number of possible patterns, nor to how abstract or concrete they can be.

What are the consequences of such a move? One difference would be that, while linguists working in other frameworks make a sharp distinction between regular and irregular morphology, such a contrast is not necessary, nor is the distinction available in any easily distinguished sense simply by culling through the data that speakers are exposed to. Speakers only hear multiple instances of forms. The only additional data that speakers have access to (in some abstract sense of 'access') is the meaning of the form (assuming they understand their interlocutors) and the frequency of the particular form. Thus, frequent irregular forms are stored in some more robust way than less frequent ones. The term normally used to describe this effect is to say that frequent forms are more highly *entrenched*. *Entrenchment* refers to the fact that some linguistic unit is stored independently. Consequently, *any* linguistic unit can be stored in such a way. As Croft and Cruse (2004: 292–3) point out, *boys* may be entrenched (hence stored as a single unit) despite the fact that it is an instance of a completely regular inflected noun. Furthermore, it may be more entrenched than a somewhat rarer irregular plural such as *oxen*. Thus, from a strictly theoretical point of view, the notion of irregular versus regular morphology has no psychological significance. It may well be that 'regular' forms get extended more frequently than 'irregular' forms, but we all know cases where irregular patterns are also extended. For example, we encounter *thunk* as a jocular past tense of *think*, or *meeses* as a jocular plural of *mice*; they are examples of extensions of rare patterns with fairly frequent occurrence. This distinction, known as the type/token contrast, will be discussed below under *Frequency*. Ultimately, therefore, much of what is traditionally thought of as a vital distinction between rule-based and memorized linguistic units has no reality in a usage-based grammar. In a usage-based grammar, only patterns for which there is evidence based on frequency of occurrence can be discovered, since there are no pre-existing innate linguistic structures to be called upon.

5.2.2 Frequency

Although it is widely believed that Chomsky (1967[1957]) definitively showed that generalized experience cannot account for ordinary human behavior, recent opinion in psychology in general, and among many linguists and psycholinguists, has turned back towards the notion that most, if not all, human learning is heavily dependent on the frequency of exposure to individual events, and that much learning can be understood as generalizations over numerous instances of experienced events.

Just as an example, Kapatsinski (2014), reviews much recent research on regular versus irregular, but patterned, allomorphy. For instance, English not only has the regular plural forms /s ~ z ~ əz/, but also irregular patterns such as /u/ʊ ~ i/ as in *tooth ~ teeth, foot ~ feet*. Although vastly outnumbered in tokens, the irregular pattern is of fairly frequent words, and consequently is overall very frequent in everyday language use. Kapatsinski shows that when confronted with novel forms, speakers not only innovate with the irregular, but frequent forms, but do so at a proportion roughly equivalent to the pattern's frequency overall in the language. For example, Kapatsinski (2014: 31) reports that he exposed English speakers to a language in which 70% of the nouns took the plural -i, and 30% took the plural -a. When presented with a new noun, the learners pluralized the new noun with -i about 70% of the time and with -a about 30% of the time.

Another somewhat surprising example of the importance of frequency in acquisition is provided by Tomasello. It is well known that the passive construction is learned quite late by English-speaking children. This fact has traditionally been cited as evidence that the construction is more complex than the active, and thus, presumably, harder to learn. In fact, there is a large, early psycholinguistic literature on the topic, which once led to the 'derivational theory of complexity', the view that constructions that were created by the application of more transformations would be more difficult to learn.[1] However, it turns out that the reason that English speakers learn passives late is because they are exposed to them much less frequently than the learners of other languages. For example, speakers of Inuktitut, K'iche', Mayan, Sesotho, and Zulu learn passives much earlier, despite similar syntactic complexity to that found in English. However, these constructions occur much more frequently in those languages than they do in English (Tomasello 2003: 173–4).

5.2.3   Emergence

A concept that has been embraced by cognitive linguists (although it's considerably older as a scientific explanatory principle—the Wikipedia entry under this term, for example, suggests references to Aristotle, John Stewart Mill, and Aldous Huxley) is emergence. Within linguistics it can be understood as the notion that complex structured behavior emerges from more elementary complex behaviors, adapted from even more elementary domains. For example, MacNeilage and his coworkers have argued that speech evolved out of the primitive sucking behavior which mammals develop in

---

[1]It should be pointed out that this theory has become irrelevant since the whole notion of 'transformation' in the generative sense is long since obsolete, but the general point still seems worth making.

the process of learning how to eat (MacNeilage and Davis 2001; MacNeilage 2008). Taking the process even earlier in human development, there is actually evidence that even such elementary behaviors as sucking and chewing are actually learned, or at least emergent, in mammals (cf. Blumberg 2006). The alternating open-close gesture of sucking and chewing corresponds, both in timing and in physiology to the alternating open-close gestures of CV syllables, which MacNeilage argues, form the framework upon which speech is built. Thus, there is no need to evoke linguistically innate structure, but rather linguistic structure *emerges* from earlier innate structures that are non-linguistic, such as suckling, or perhaps even heartbeat.

To put it somewhat contentiously, there are no innate linguistic structures, but rather linguistic structures are learned from numerous instances, scaffolded upon pre-existing non-linguistic structures that are themselves probably scaffolded on strictly physiological mechanisms that are probably the only true candidates for innateness.

At the syntactic level, on the other hand, construction grammarians have argued that general syntactic patterns (even those as general as the iconic 'S —> NP + VP') emerge from generalization of more lexically specific patterns. Hoffman (2017)'s analysis of *refuse* discussed in Chap. 4, for example, illustrates this point.

As was stated above, Tomasello argues that children build increasingly abstract syntactic patterns from more specific ones through a gradual process in which constructions are first lexically-specific, then generalized to semantically-defined verb classes, only to schematize further to something like the level of generality in a generative grammar late in the language acquisition process. This kind of abstraction (the building of abstract notions from concrete examples) through 'bootstrapping' renders unnecessary any notion of innate *syntactic* structures or frameworks beyond the innate ability to generalize/schematize over multiple instances, and then to schematize over schemas.

Schemas are initially fixed expressions with slots (recalling tagmemic concepts, or old-fashioned language-learning exercises). Further examples similar to those discussed above can be found in Tomasello's work (2003: 148–149). He cites examples like

1 It's a/the X (identification function)
2 Here's a/the X (attributive function)
3 That's my/Y's X (possessive function)

which are, at the beginning, the majority type of utterance that children hear, and which provide the framework through which the category Noun may emerge.

While children learn many transitive verbs at an early stage (*get, have, want, take, find, put*), it appears that they do not generalize to a transitive NP V NP pattern until relatively late in the language acquisition process, around 3 1/2 (Tomasello 2003: 150). What does this mean overall? It means that the schema S —> NP + VP emerges as a generalization over numerous instances of various kinds of subjects combining with various kinds of predicates, which themselves emerge from various kinds of verbs combining with various kinds of objects (or not). There is no need to posit language-specific schemas (even those as general as Merge) when the ability to schematize through numerous related instances, coupled with the memory of large numbers of those instances, can lead to grammatical patterning that is as powerful as (and not more powerful than) context-free phrase structure grammars (Chomsky 1957).

5.2.4 First Language Acquisition

If, as we saw in a previous section, we do not assume that the rules of generative grammar are what speakers either learn or use, we are forced back upon language acquisition based solely on the data available to the learner, i.e. *usage-based* acquisition. Tomasello puts it this way:

> children do not first learn words and then combine them into sentences via contentless syntactic "rules." Rather, children learn simultaneously from adult utterances meaningful linguistic structures of many shapes and sizes and degrees of abstraction, and they then produce their own utterances on particular occasions of use by piecing together some of these many and variegated units in ways that express their immediate communicative intention. (Tomasello 2003: 99–100)

Continuing with the theme of what children are exposed to, Tomasello notes that a very large number of the utterances children hear are essentially patterns with blanks, which he calls *frames*. These include instances such as *Are you..., It's..., Can you...?, Let's..., Look at..., What did...?* (Tomasello 2003: 110). These frames serve two roles simultaneously. They enable the construction of novel utterances without the need for the acquisition of abstract rules. And secondly, they enable the acquisition of new lexical items, as each new instance of an already existing frame with a new lexical filler provides an item that can be added to the set of 'things that fit into that slot'. In some instances, this can even serve as the genesis of a lexical category such as Verb or Noun.

An even more interesting consequence of this view of acquisition through the storage and generalization of frames is that many of what appear to be general rules are actually initially quite lexically specific. For example, many verbs are used only in specific contexts in child-directed speech, and thus presumably are acquired initially as specific frames. Tomasello uses the example of *cut*, which is only used with a simple direct object, but *draw* is used with more complex frames, such as *draw X, draw X on Y, X draw on Y*. "Interestingly and importantly, within any given verb's development there was great continuity such that new uses of a given verb almost always replicated previous uses and then made one small addition or modification (such as the marking of tense or the adding of a new argument)" (Tomasello 2003: 117). Thus, the acquisition of syntactic patterns is gradual and initially lexically specific. The traditional generative understanding of rules is not compatible with this kind of acquisition. And a further and perhaps less commented-upon consequence is that this view requires either that adult language is simply a bigger version of this pattern, or that at some stage people completely reorganize their internal grammars by discarding all the existing patterns and replacing them with rules. But nobody has ever suggested that such a monumental cognitive re-upholstering ever takes place. Small-scale reorganizations of irregular verb or noun patterns have been observed, but the wholesale abandonment of frames in favor of rules does not appear to occur at any stage of language acquisition up to adulthood. Since we know that children do learn syntax (and probably morphology as well) via the generalization of recurrent patterns, there is no need to posit abstract rules that have no inherent content, and whose form is so unsemantic that they must be innate.

5.2.5 Second Language Acquisition

Within the framework of Cognitive Linguistics, second language acquisition is not considered as different in kind from children's acquisition of their first language (Achard and Niemeier 2008 and papers in that volume). Both are usage-based, with children and second language learners expanding their linguistic production as their mental data grow through observation (a term used broadly here) of language use in others around them and, for the latter group, through direct instruction and linguistic modeling. This usage-based view of second language acquisition broadly informs second language pedagogy. More specifically, it sheds light on the way in which learners acquire narrowly employed lexical items and even grammatical structures. They expand their linguistic mastery as they are exposed to further meanings and to extensions of constructions to wider contexts.

The notion of the radial set can play a role in the expansion of second language proficiency. Students may acquire new meanings of polysemous units by being exposed to them indirectly as they read or practice guided conversations, or even directly when connections are pointed out by the instructor. The study of idioms is often shaped by an awareness (tacit or explicit) of metaphorical language. Both categorization (underlying the radial semantic set) and the pervasive existence of metaphor and metonymy figure in second-language acquisition, all of which, especially for adult languages, is shaped by an emerging meta-categorization of what belong in one's first language and what is part of the language being acquired.

5.3 Sociolinguistics

In the mid 2000's cognitive linguists began considering sociolinguistic issues in their studies. This is a natural result of the insistence on the emphasis on language use. Language use, as opposed to the more traditional 'armchair' study of Language, forces the investigator to consider the existence of variation, which, as has been known since the work of Labov and others in the mid-sixties, is structured and linguistically significant. One result has been "the incorporation of factors relating to the pragmatic context of language use in the description of linguistic phenomena that are of specific interest to Cognitive Linguistics" (Kristiansen and Geeraerts 2013: 2), while the other is "the reverse perspective, i.e. the introduction of a cognitive linguistic perspective into the study of lectal and contextual variation" (p. 2). Geeraerts and Kristiansen (2015: 369–370) put it as follows:

> Cognitive Linguistics adopts a usage-based model of language…individual usage events are realizations of an existing systemic structure, but at the same time, it is only through the individual usage events that changes might be introduced into the structure. 'System', in fact, is primarily an observable commonality in the behavior of language users, and as such, it is the result of social interaction. People influence each other's linguistic behavior, basically by co-operative imitation and adaptation, and, in some cases, by opposition and a desire for distinctiveness.

Several interesting sociolinguistic studies that call on Cognitive Linguistic concepts can illustrate this development. For example, Nycz (2013) studied the English of speakers of Canadian English who moved to New York City. Canadian English exhibits two striking phonological features that distinguish it from most varieties of American English, and specifically from the English of the North-East US, such as is found in New York.

Canadian English is marked by the presence of the celebrated rule of Canadian Raising, the presence of raised allophones of the /ai/ and /au/ diphthongs before voiceless consonants (in, for example, *right* and *about*). Thus, *right* and *ride* have different vowels, as do *lout* and *loud*, although the difference is arguably allophonic. The second feature is what has come to be known as the 'low-back merger'. The historically-distinct vowels in *caught* and *cot* are kept contrastive in the Eastern half of the United States, but have merged in the Western half of the US to /ɑ/. However, in Canada they have merged instead to /ɒ/, a low back rounded vowel. Thus, in Canada *cod* and *cawed* have identical vowels, but in New York they do not.

Canadians who have moved to New York would be expected to accommodate to their surroundings, and thus, presumably, to lose these two distinctive Canadian speech features. However, the way in which they might be lost would bear on which model of linguistic processing is assumed. A rule-based model (such as generative phonology) would assume that the loss of raising would be gradual, but should not affect words differently, as it is the loss of an allophonic rule, and thus should apply equally to all words in its domain. On the other hand, the *unmerging* of the low back vowel should be expected to be all or none phonetically, but *lexically* gradual, as each word is relexified with the appropriate vowel. However, what Nycz found was that most speakers exhibited a small but significant phonetic difference between *cot* and *caught* in conversational speech after phonological factors have been accounted for. Frequency effects, consistent with a lexically gradual divergence of these two vowel categories, were found, as would be expected in a usage-based theory (Nycz 2013: 59). However, there was much less change in the amount of Canadian Raising produced, although the change was again, gradual, and also lexically-marked (specifically, *out* and *about* were the words most likely to continue exhibiting raising).[2] Nycz suggests that this is in accord with a usage-based model of storage and

---

[2]Also interesting, although tangential to this discussion, is the fact that these changes happened at all. In many contexts Canadians (at least those in the eastern half of the country) take pains to

processing, in that it is assumed that social as well as phonetic information is stored with each lexical item. Canadian Raising is a distinctive and highly salient aspect of Canadian English, while the low back merger is normally completely unremarked. Note that this 'invisibility' of the low back merger is true not only for Canadian English, but also for American English. While most Americans are aware of dialect differences across the US, they are normally totally unaware that West of the Mississippi *cot* and *caught* have merged, although they are well aware of other characteristic phonological features such as New York's 'toity-toid' and Southern Smoothing (the stereotyped monophthongization of the /ai/ phoneme in *my, eye*).

Nycz (2013: 52) summarizes the view of how sound change spreads within a usage-based model as follows: "In usage-based models, the process of "losing" a rule is much more gradual: change occurs on a word-by-word basis, not through the alteration of a single rule. More frequent items will acquire new dialect exemplars at a faster rate than low frequency items, with the result that productions of high frequency words should be the first to shift."

Overall, it is clear that the usage-based, cognitive model of language structure comes with a built-in mechanism to account for sociolinguistic behavior (such as variable outputs and sensitivity to social and other cultural context), in that each stored unit includes information about its social marking status, thus making that information available to the speaker at the point of choosing a particular utterance in a particular context.

5.4 Poetics and Literary Theory

An area of study and analysis that fits naturally within the Cognitive Linguistics domain is literary theory, at least in part because two essential tools of purely linguistic analysis, metaphor and conceptual blending, are also literary devices of long standing. Tsur (2002: 2) puts it well when he says: "poetry exploits, for aesthetic purposes, cognitive (including linguistic) processes that were initially evolved for non-aesthetic purposes, just as in evolving linguistic ability, old cognitive and physiological mechanisms were turned to new ends." In other words, we can use the mechanisms developed to analyze Language to analyze literary and poetic language, since the medium, Language, is the same object. Freeman (2006: 2) phrases the issue as follows: "Linguistics contributes scientific explanations for the findings of literary critics and thus provides a means whereby their knowledge and insights might be seen in the context of a unified theory of human cognition and language."

To illustrate, one issue that has been heavily debated within literary theory is the question of the 'voice' or perspective of the 'author'. Freeman suggests that the notion of construal (see Chap. 3 for discussion) can be fruitfully applied to an

---

differentiate themselves from United States residents. One could imagine their maintaining these distinctive raised vowels as a very linguistic form of differentiation.

understanding of the perspective taken by the author, and further, and perhaps more interestingly, by the reader.

Another obvious area where there is a confluence between strictly linguistic and literary views of linguistic devices is in the area of metaphor itself. It has been argued that "poetic thought uses the mechanisms of everyday thought. It extends them, however, elaborates them, and combines them in ways that go beyond the ordinary" (Lakoff and Turner 1989: 67). Freeman (p. 9) points out that it is not sufficient to argue that literary metaphors are 'just' metaphors like those explored in Lakoff and Johnson's pivotal book, but that instead "a continuum exists between creative and conventional use of metaphor, and that devices such as elaboration, extension, and compression account for the distinction between them."

Another illustration of the confluence of Cognitive Linguistics and literary analysis using the notion of blends can be found in Brandt's analysis of Edna St. Vincent Millay's *First Fig*:

4 My candle burns at both ends;
   It will not last the night;
   But ah, my foes, and oh, my friends –
   It gives a lovely light!

The Brandts (2017) show that Millay constructs a blended space of living that includes both the conventional trope of a candle burning at both ends and her overblown lifestyle, the blend leading to the conclusion that her behavior is both dangerous and thrilling. As the Brandts put it: "although this is known and accepted [viz: that burning the candle at both ends halves its useful life], it is nevertheless better to double-burn the candle – in the context of foes and friends – for a new reason. Double consumption of energy yields double effect in these respects, so foes will be more forcefully attacked, and friends will be more intensely delighted, although for a shorter time" (p. 118).

5.5 Conclusions

With this chapter we have laid out some of the aspects of Cognitive Linguistics which are attracting the most attention at present, among them extensions to sociolinguistics and poetics. The most important, perhaps, are those (emergence, the role of frequency, the whole notion of a usage-based theory) which are making strong claims about the nature of the human mind. If we were to make predictions (never really safe in social and behavioral sciences), we would foresee even greater attention to those aspects of Cognitive Linguistics which shed light on the cognitive side. Linguists are already using both increased psycholinguistic methodology and the emerging tools of corpora and big data analysis to move forward our understanding of Language and the mind.

References

Achard, M., and S. Niemeyer. 2008. Cognitive linguistics, language acquisition and pedagogy. In *Cognitive linguistics, second language acquisition, and foreign language teaching*, ed. M. Achard and S. Niemeyer, 1–12. Berlin/New York: de Gruyter Mouton.

Blumberg, M.S. 2006. *Basic instinct: The genesis of behavior*. New York: Basic Books.

Brandt, L., and P.A. Brandt. 2017. Cognitive poetics and imagery. *European Journal of English Studies* 9 (2): 117–130.

Chomsky, N. 1957. *Syntactic structures*. Janua linguarum, IV. The Hague: Mouton.

Chomsky, N. 1967[1957]. A review of B.F. Skinner's *Verbal behavior*. In *Readings in the psychology of language*, ed. L.A. Jakobovits and M.S. Miron, 142–143. Englewood Cliffs, NJ: Prentice-Hall.

Croft, W., and D.A. Cruse. 2004. *Cognitive linguistics*. Cambridge textbooks in linguistics. Cambridge, UK: Cambridge University Press.

Freeman, M.H. 2006. From metaphor to iconicity in a poetic text. In *The metaphors of sixty: Papers presented on the occasion of the 60th birthday of Zoltán Kövecses*, ed. R. Benczes and S. Csábi, 127–135. Budapest: Eötvös Loránd University.

Geeraerts, D., and G. Kristiansen. 2015. Variationist linguistics. In *Handbook of cognitive linguistics*, ed. E. Dąbrowska and D. Divjak, 366–389. Berlin/New York: de Gruyter Mouton.

Hoffman, T. 2017. Construction grammars. In *The Cambridge handbook of cognitive linguistics*, ed. B. Dancygier, 310–329. Cambridge, UK: Cambridge University Press.

Kapatsinski, V. 2014. What is grammar like? A usage-based constructionist perspective. *Linguistic Issues in Language Technology* 11 (1): 1–41.

Kristiansen, G., and D. Geeraerts. 2013. Contexts and usage in cognitive sociolinguistics. *Journal of Pragmatics* 52: 1–4.

Lakoff, G., and M. Turner. 1989. *More than cool reason: A field guide to poetic metaphor*. Chicago: University of Chicago Press.

Langacker, R.W. 1988. A usage-based model. In *Topics in cognitive linguistics*, ed. B. Rudzka-Ostyn, 127–161. Amsterdam/Philadelphia: Benjamins.

MacNeilage, P. 2008. *The origin of speech*. Oxford/New York: Oxford University Press.

MacNeilage, P.F., and B.L. Davis. 2001. Motor mechanisms in speech ontogeny: Phylogenetic, neurobiological and linguistic implications. *Current Opinion in Neurobiology* 11: 696–700.

Nycz, J. 2013. Changing words or changing rules? Second dialect acquisition and phonological representation. *Journal of Pragmatics* 52: 49–62.

Tomasello, M. 2003. *Constructing a language: A usage-based theory of language acquisition*. Cambridge, MA: Harvard University Press.

Tsur, R. 2002. *Aspects of cognitive poetics*. Retrieved from https://www2.bc.edu/~richarad/lcb/fea/tsur/cogpoetics.html.

Chapter 6
Conclusions

6.1 Summary

As was stated in the Preface, this monograph does not have as a goal to change minds about linguistic theory. Rather, we have laid out Cognitive Linguistics as a response to two realities. First, the theory has grown widely in scope and in the number of practitioners since it was developed, both in North America and Europe in the 1980s. The first Cognitive Linguistics conference, held in 1981, attracted some 80 participants, while the most recent ones are attended by nearly a thousand linguists and students of linguistics from around the world. There are now book series, journals, multiple annual and biennial conferences devoted to the theory or to one or another of its subcomponents. Secondly, too many of us tend to be attached to our own theoretical outlook to the exclusion of others. We believe that theories can interact and, in doing so, help to clarify analyses in ways that narrower approaches might miss. There is a need to understand what others are doing, both for our research and for the training of the next generation of linguists in the classroom and during periods of supervision.

With our audience of practicing linguists in mind, we have taken a somewhat chronological approach to this monograph, mirroring in some ways how Cognitive Linguistics has developed and how it was discovered by many of us who work in the framework. This volume, therefore, begins with an overview of the sources of the theory, from both sides of the Atlantic, and a short history of how its name evolved, not totally without controversy. The second chapter treats the earliest work to appear, work which caught the imagination of many of us and led us to our own research projects. The next two chapters set out the core of Cognitive Linguistics, first through an overview of its theoretical commitments and then through a selection of case studies. Finally, Chap. 5 returns to chronology, providing a view into new approaches to the theory and new ways in which its application has been widened.

75
M. E. Winters and G. S. Nathan, *Cognitive Linguistics for Linguists*,
Expert Briefs, https://doi.org/10.1007/978-3-030-33604-2_6

6.2 Outstanding Questions

Throughout this volume, one of the themes (perhaps better to think of it as a meta-theme) being explored is that Cognitive Linguistics is a unified theory. This unification takes several forms, of which one is the continuum of meaningful units from morphemes to complex grammatical structures. This claim is not a new one; Langacker (1987), among others, made it from the time of the earliest explorations. "There is no meaningful distinction between grammar and lexicon. Lexicon, morphology, and syntax form a continuum of symbolic structures, which differ along various parameters but can be divided into separate components only arbitrarily" (p. 3).

Further kinds of unification have followed. Other early papers (cf. Chap. 2) extended prototype theory within what was then still a nascent approach to language change across the lexicon and grammar. Other work on metaphor has overlapped with philosophical considerations of mathematics (Lakoff and Núñez 2000) and political discourse (Musolff 2017). Chapter 4, in an additional extension, has a discussion of one of the ways in which phonology can be studied within this framework, making use of many of the same theoretical entities that have been brought into play for directly meaningful units. Finally, as discussed in Chap. 5, the theory can be usefully applied to fields as divergent as sociolinguistics and poetics.

We do not want to imply, however, that all linguistic puzzles have now been solved. In the following paragraphs we will discuss two areas which need much further exploration. The first is, perhaps, best viewed as theory-internal, that is, the relationship as stated explicitly in Cognitive Linguistics between meaning and form. The second has broader implications since it arises in other theories as well; we will point out some of the questions which emerge when overarching explanations are proposed.

6.2.1 Syntax/Semantics Mapping

From the beginning, one of the undisputed tenets of Cognitive Linguistics has been the relationship between grammar and meaning, clearly stated by Langacker (1987: 2): "Grammar (or syntax) does not constitute an autonomous formal level of representation. Instead, grammar is symbolic in nature, consisting in the conventional symbolization of semantic structure." We can discern two challenges to more mainstream beliefs in this statement. First is the challenge to the autonomy of syntax, a position that has been explored and, to some extent, disproven in the intervening years (cf., for example, Anderson 2015). The second, that grammar is symbolic, has become a given, a primitive of cognitive theory. It has not, however, been established or falsified by independent means.

It is difficult, in fact, to see how the universal mapping of syntax on semantics can be proven; there would have to be a demonstration that there are no exceptions across all dialects and across all times in the history of these dialects. While one can argue that words and compounds may be exceptionlessly meaningful, grammatical morphemes and larger grammatical structures present more of a challenge. In theory, any one example of a meaningless unit would falsify this commitment, but there is the question of how one judges lack of meaning, especially within a theory that holds to a very broad definition, going far beyond any dictionary entry or, at times, usage. Demonstrating the universal semantic content of grammar, both for larger expressions and for subcomponents, is work still to be accomplished.

6.2.2 Explanatory Approaches

In the last decade or so, as was discussed in Chap. 5, frequency has been adduced as virtually the sole explanation for prototype formation, diachronic change, and acquisition; Bybee (2007: 980–991) is a clear statement of this point of view. Some work, however, has pointed out that this is not the only way of looking at motivations (cf. Winters 2010 on salience and Nathan 2008, 2017 on naturalness). They are discussed briefly here to underline the need to look for multiple explanatory processes and entities rather than relying on a single motivating force.

6.2.2.1 Salience and Frequency

The key question which follows from the claim that frequency is the most funda-mental explanation for language function (synchronic and diachronic) is where the frequency comes from. What, that is, causes some unit to be more frequent than others? Part of the answer lies in the pragmatics end of the meaning continuum; babies acquiring language, for example, have as input frequently repeated phrases from their care-givers mirroring their baby lives. Not all items derive their frequency from pragmatic situations, however. Winters (2010) suggests that cultural salience may be another contribution; in illustrations found in elementary reading textbooks in the United States, which often depict idealized families in suburban homes with yards, the bird standing on the lawn is a robin. It is the case that robins do not neces-sarily live in cities (sparrows would be the most frequent bird), but they are identified by many North Americans as a result of exposure to these readers and other images as the prototypical bird. Actual frequency is not a factor, but salience is.[1] For other reasons, inhabitants of Japan, as was mentioned in Chap. 3, would pick out the crane as prototypical, not because they exist in large numbers in Japan, but because of their cultural and spiritual significance.

---

[1] It was a matter of some controversy in 1964 when the Disney movie of *Mary Poppins* was released. When Mary sings about a robin the scene cuts to an American robin singing, but, of course, as linguists know, the British robin is a different bird, and looks very different. Those familiar with British robins were furious.

One could argue, however, that physical existence is not the only kind of frequency which leads to language acquisition and change. Cranes are, in some respect, very frequent in Japanese sensibility despite their non-existence outside of zoos and other artificial habitats. Robins, the same way, may be cognitively frequent precisely because they are presented as the standard bird in readers. What seems to be the case is that we have a 'chicken and egg' question here. Does salience lead to frequency or does frequency lead to salience? The answer is surely not an absolute one, but rather may be a matter of individual units. Again, as with the semantics of all grammatical units, more work is called for, taking into consideration the formation of semantic sets, language acquisition, and diachronic processes.

6.2.2.2   The Role of Naturalness

When we look at phonology and the nature of sounds and their organization, another explanatory factor may well replace frequency in importance. As Nathan (2015, 2017) has argued, sounds are not just meaningful mental symbols (although one might argue that phonemes are), but rather the product of human physiology, both articulatory and acoustic. In short, we make the sounds we do because of the way we are; there is no language, for example, with an apico-uvular trill since our tongues are not engineered to bend back on themselves so that the tip touches the back of the soft palate. In the same way, /h/ disappears over time (and in dialect variation) in a wide range of unrelated languages because the sound is hard to hear, particularly in normal or fast speech.

As with the relationship between salience and frequency, the relationship between sounds and physiology is a complex one. It is difficult to decide a priori whether what might be called naturalness (human characteristics such as the shape of our vocal tract or our ability to differentiate sounds because of our aural apparatus) leads to frequency or if even physiological facts can be better understood in the context of frequency.

Naturalness is probably also a factor in other realms of grammar. For example, the work of McWhorter (2018) argues that there are cognitively motivated simplification strategies that apply to morphological systems, leading to similarities across unrelated creole languages around the world. Similarly, Chambers (2004) argues that there are universal paths of simplification in non-standard dialects of the same language across different languages with standard and non-standard dialects, similarly pointing to cognitively-based simplification strategies. There needs to be additional attention paid to the idea that naturalness, as understood, for example, by the Natural Phonologists is motivated not by UG, but rather by the fact that Language is spoken through physical and general cognitive means. These means are constrained by physiology and perception, and physical and cognitive effort must be a factor influencing linguistic systems not only in phonology but in other domains that call upon cognitive effort to implement. This will lead to universal simplification strategies. Furthermore, additional effort in speaking, to clarify or emphasize, would explain widely shared patterns of emphasis and clarification found around the world. Again, further study is required here.

6.3   Relationship to Contemporary Theories

Although Cognitive Linguistics is a robust and growing field of research, it is probably still at a minimum second in position to the prototypical formal theory, currently referred to as Minimalism. Minimalism continues to maintain the traditional view of Language as a formal system whose nature is unlearnable and must therefore be innate. This view includes (extremely simplified) phrase structure rules ('merge') and similarly simplified transformations ('move') along with constraints on both. Current references include Radford (2004), van Gelderen (2017), Bošković and Lasnik (2006), Chomsky (2014). There is very little in common with most of the commitments of Cognitive Linguistics.

On the other hand, other more formally-oriented syntactic theories share certain worldviews with current Cognitive Linguistics. For example, Head-Driven Phrase Structure Grammar (HPSG) (Pollard and Sag 1994; Levine 2017) assumes the existence of simple phrase structure rules, but has rich lexical representations that dictate which words can be combined into phrases with others, and rules that generate new lexical representations permitting much of what can be captured through 'transformations' without reorganizing actual sentences. This approach is similar to Langacker's understanding of 'inheritance' and 'construal'.

Another contemporary syntactic theory (more correctly, morphosyntactic, as morphology has begun to be assimilated into the theory as well) is Lexical-Functional Grammar (LFG). Like HPSG, LFG is a monostratal theory (each sentence has only one phrase structure), but there are additional structures simultaneously associated with each sentence. There is, however, no derivational relationship between the associated representations. In recent years, however, LFG has been strongly influenced by usage-based theories (Bresnan 2007; Ford and Bresnan 2015). Bresnan has been using corpus data to explore probabilistic explanations for constraints on 'dative movement' (showing, incidentally, that there are semantic differences between the variants) (Bresnan 2007) and exploring experimental methods for generating corpus data for languages and constructions for which there are not sufficient existing data. More recently she has been studying ways in which the lexicon can contain items that do not correspond exactly with sentence constituents, such as *Where's* in *Where's my pants* (Bresnan, p.c.).

Within formal phonology the almost total triumph of Optimality Theory (McCarthy 2004, 2008) has introduced the possibility of a connection with usage-based models. Boersma and others have suggested that the constraints in OT grammars might be probabilistic and that learning, even of phonological categories such as 'features,' might be usage based (Boersma et al. 2003).

6.4   Concluding Remarks

We hope we have been able to present Cognitive Linguistics as a coherent and fruitful research program. We believe it has provided insights into the nature of human language that have not been captured by other, more autonomous theories. Even if the program is not adopted wholesale by the entire linguistic community, it will, we believe, continue to provide additional data and analyses that other OWLs, 'ordinary working linguists' (as coined by Charles Fillmore) will find useful.

References

Anderson, J.M. 2015. The non-autonomy of syntax. *Folia Linguistica* 39: 223–250.

Boersma, P., P. Escudero, and R. Hayes. (2003). Learning abstract phonological from auditory phonetic categories: An integrated model for the acquisition of language-specific sound categories. In *International congress of phonetic sciences*, 1013–1016. Retrieved from https://www. internationalphoneticassociation.org/icphs-proceedings/ICPhS2003/p15_1013.html.

Bošković, Z., and H. Lasnik. 2006. *Minimalist syntax: The essential readings*. Malden, MA/Oxford: Wiley-Blackwell.

Bresnan, J. 2007. Is syntactic knowledge probabilistic? Experiments with the English dative construction. In *Roots: Linguistics in search of its evidential base*, ed. S. Featherston and W. Steinfeld, 75–96. Berlin/Boston: de Gruyter Mouton.

Bybee, J. 2007. Diachronic linguistics. In *The Oxford handbook of cognitive linguistics*, ed. D. Geeraerts and H. Cuyckens, 945–987. Oxford/New York: Oxford University Press.

Chambers, J. 2004. Dynamic typology and vernacular universals. In *Dialectology meets typology*, ed. B. Kortmann, 127–145. Berlin/New York: de Gruyter Mouton.

Chomsky, N. 2014. *The minimalist program*. Cambridge, MA: MIT Press.

Ford, M., and J. Bresnan. 2015. Generating data as a proxy for unavailable corpus data: The contextualized sentence completion task. *Corpus Linguistics and Linguistic Theory* 11 (1): 187–224.

Lakoff, G., and R.E. Núñez. 2000. *Where mathematics comes from: How the embodied mind brings mathematics into being*. New York: Basic Books.

Langacker, R.W. 1987. *Foundations of cognitive grammar, Volume 1, Theoretical prerequisites*. Stanford: Stanford University Press.

Levine, R.D. 2017. *Syntactic analysis: An HPSG-based approach*. Cambridge, UK: Cambridge University Press.

McCarthy, J.J. (ed.). 2004. *Optimality theory in phonology: A reader*. Malden, MA/Oxford: Blackwell.

McCarthy, J.J. 2008. *Doing optimality theory: Applying theory to data*. Malden, MA/Oxford: Blackwell.

McWhorter, J.H. 2018. *The creole debate*. Cambridge, UK: Cambridge University Press.

Musolff, A. 2017. Truth, lies and figurative scenarios: Metaphors at the heart of Brexit. *Journal of Language and Politics* 16: 641–657.

Nathan, G.S. 2008. *Phonology: A cognitive grammar introduction*. Amsterdam/Philadelphia: Benjamins.

Nathan, G.S. 2015. Phonology. In *Handbook of cognitive linguistics*, ed. E. Dąbrowska and D. Divjak, 253–273. Berlin/New York: de Gruyter Mouton.

Nathan, G.S. 2017. Phonology. In *Handbook of cognitive linguistics*, ed. B. Dancygier, 252–273. Cambridge, UK: Cambridge University Press.

Pollard, C., and I.A. Sag. 1994. *Head-driven phrase structure grammar. Studies in contemporary linguistics*. Stanford: Center for the Study of Language and Information; Chicago: University of Chicago Press.

Radford, A. 2004. *Minimalist syntax*. Cambridge, UK: Cambridge University Press.

van Gelderen, E. 2017. *Syntax: An introduction to minimalism*. Amsterdam/Philadelphia: Benjamins.

Winters, M.E. 2010. Linguistic categories and language change. In *English language, literature and culture: New directions in research*, ed. C. Humphries, J. Kossek, and A. Gomola, Bielsko-Bialo: ATH.

Winters, M.E. 2012. Grammatical meaning and the old French subjunctive. In *Research on old French: The state of the art*, ed. D.L. Arteaga, 351–376. Dordrecht: Springer.

CPSIA information can be obtained
at www.ICGtesting.com
Printed in the USA
LVHW081721050120
642562LV00005B/46/P